GET THE F*CK OUT YOUR OWN WAY

GET THE F*CK OUT YOUR OWN WAY

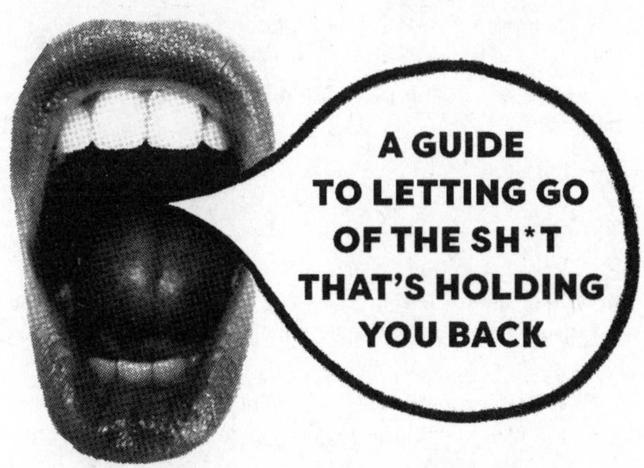

MJ HARRIS

LEGACY
LIT
NEW YORK BOSTON

Legacy Lit
Hachette Book Group
1290 Avenue of the Americas
New York, NY 10104
LegacyLitBooks.com
Twitter.com/LegacyLitBooks
Instagram.com/LegacyLitBooks

First Edition: January 2024

Legacy Lit is an imprint of Grand Central Publishing. The Legacy Lit name and logo are trademarks of Hachette Book Group, Inc.

Library of Congress Cataloging-in-Publication Data
Names: Harris, M J (Lifystyle and business influencer), author.
Title: Get the f*ck out your own way : a guide to letting go of the sh*t that's holding you back / MJ Harris.
Other titles: Get the fuck out your own way
Description: First edition. | New York : Legacy Lit, 2024.
Identifiers: LCCN 2023036402 | ISBN 9780306829222 (hardcover) | ISBN 9780306829246 (ebook)
Subjects: LCSH: Self-actualization (Psychology) | Self-realization. | Goal (Psychology)
Classification: LCC BF637.S4 H363 2024 | DDC 158.1—dc23/eng/20230804
LC record available at https://lccn.loc.gov/2023036402

ISBNs: 9780306829222 (hardcover), 9780306829246 (ebook)

Printed in the United States of America

LSC-C

Printing 1, 2023

This book is dedicated to you—every person who over the last fifteen years has invited me into your hearts, homes, and phones. Your love and support are a blessing to me, and my heart's desire is to be a continued blessing to you. Love you.

CONTENTS

CONTENTS

GET THE F*CK OUT YOUR OWN WAY

INTRODUCTION

Don't Be Original, Be Effective

New Year, New Me. Ain't that what's going through the minds of everyone when that clock hits midnight each year and catapults us into a new dawn?

A new dawn. A new sun. And underneath that sun... possibilities. The new you just waitin' to be seen.

I say bull. And if you're reading this on any day other than December 31st, I bet you know the other half of that word.

Hold on. Lemme back you up real fast now and tell you the first piece of advice you have come to seek by opening up this book: *Honey, there ain't nothing new under the sun.*

Stare at it, soak it in, memorize it until your eyes get crossed, because it ain't going nowhere. Slam the book shut and toss it aside, but I bet you will come back. Those words, they bite. They itch. Like chicken pox. They will not quit until you figure it out. Well, read on because I am about to lay down the law.

I wish I could take the credit for this phrase, but that would mean crossing my biggest source of motivation, and I ain't about to do that. And no, it is not just because she is my mother and I want to stay on her good side.

The first time my mother said this phrase to me was when I got into trouble at school. She came to pick me up, and she stared at me with that look parents get in their eyes. You know, *that* look. And she went: "Did you do that?"

Of course I said no. Ain't no kid ever give up that easy. I said, "I have my own version of what happened."

My mother, she saw right through that. She got this look, and she said, "There ain't nothing new under the sun. I know what you're doing."

And I tell you, I ain't ever had my hopes come crashin' down so fast before. Those words, they hit me in my gut like nothing before. But then, you know what? They *stuck* with me. Maybe that was because my mother repeated them so often—which was my own fault—but whatever the case, they grew with me. They started small, but the older I got, the more expansive they became.

They became my *motivation*.

Motivation, I tell you, is one hell of a drug. As I got older and experienced new things and new obstacles, her words would come back to me every time I slipped or did not know where to go or what to do. Even better, her phrase implied something else: If there ain't nothing new under the sun, then I could stop beatin' my head against the wall trying to figure everything out for myself; I could just find out how somebody else did it and make it work for me, too.

If you are wondering how on God's green earth this applies to you, then buckle down and listen up. You picked this book up for one reason: Ya need help! Financial help, spiritual help, relationship help, career help—whatever it is, you need it. You need empowerment. You need direction. But you do *not* need a new you. And what's more, there ain't a new you waiting in the New Year. But there *is* a fresh, new perspective you can take with you, courtesy of yours truly.

The earth has been spinning round the sun for billions of years and there are very few new things left to pop up these days, so don't try to be original.

Instead—BE EFFECTIVE.

Find what works for other people in your situation and glean from that to get to where you want to get. No matter your situation or challenge, know that someone somewhere out there has already been through it before. Has *survived* it. Has mastered it. Has kicked that good-for-nothing strife out the goddamn roof! There is nothing unique about it.

Millions of people have gone through the exact same thing that you're going through right now, and your victory will have nothing new or unique about it. If you're sad about that, get over it. Why are you sad when you should be relieved? Be *relieved* that the heavy lifting was done before you, that numerous paths have been carved out—you just gotta find the one for you. There is victory out there; there is hope. There are solutions. So get up, use what I'm about to say, and do the work you gotta do.

There's nothing new under the sun. Once you realize that, you can shorten the time it takes to do anything—and you can start today. Begin your new business. Do the work to overcome the challenges in your relationship, with your family, or with your friends. But just *start.* There's nothing that you're experiencing—positive or negative—that someone else has not already experienced.

When you start, you'll notice that all the people who share a story like yours—as well as those who do not—have all done one thing. They *told* their story, in one way, shape, or form. They did not hide that trauma. Getting the fuck out your own way requires that you open up. You heard me, open it all up!

I am not saying you gotta take a bullhorn and scream your story, but whatever avenue or path makes you feel good, take it. Just get it out into the open, off your chest and outta your mind. Because keeping our cards close—keeping our trauma to ourselves—is the worst thing we can do. When we do, we prevent ourselves from building connection through vulnerability. More importantly, we prevent *ourselves* from being able to leverage other people's lessons of how they got through it to get through our own trauma. And I know, honey, I know—that temptation is hard to resist, the temptation to clam up and not tell a soul what we've really been through. But if I can do it, you can, too.

You know, I grew up in the South, surrounded by a culture where no one airs their dirty laundry. Hell, no one aired *any* laundry because it was not anyone else's business. Keep it shut. Stay quiet. That was the mantra, and had it not been for my mother, I would be in a much worse place than I am. This book might not even exist. She was very transparent about everything. She told me, "If you share your story with folks, it takes away the shame from you." The only way that shame can exist is when something is a secret. It can only exist in secrecy. And when you share it, it takes away that power. And when you take away the shame that you associate with your story, you realize that there is *nothing* wrong with your story. *This* is your story. It is painful, but there is nothing to be ashamed of.

I'm sharing *my* story here with you because I don't want anyone or anything, including my *own* story, to have any power over me, just like you shouldn't want anyone or anything to have power over you. Our secrets suffocate us because they make us believe that we're alone. They make us believe that we're abnormal. They make us believe that there's something *wrong* with us. I was inspired to share my story, as an act of faith, believing that if I shared my own lessons with you there'll be some people in the world who raise their hand to be able to say, "I'm just like you." And even if it's just a couple people, at the very least I wouldn't have to be alone in my story anymore.

So, if we can open ourselves to the idea of sharing our story with people who we deem to be safe and deserving of that information, we can learn to evolve and grow away from what we've been through—and what we're going through every day. One of the things that keeps us traumatized and keeps us bitter is that we don't open up and tell anyone anything. And that prevents us from being able to build connection through vulnerability—more importantly, it prevents us from being able to leverage other people's lessons of how they got through it to get through shit for ourselves.

So, you ready? Leverage what I am about to say—leverage what you can from the next eighteen chapters, and remember, if and when the lesson applies to you, use it! Take the knowledge I'm sharing and leverage it to the best of your ability because there ain't nothing new. You just need to find out how somebody else did it because there ain't nothing new under the sun. The sooner we realize that, the sooner we get our heads back on straight. Your time is so much more valuable than for you to just sit under the sun and wait for a new you when all you have to do is open your eyes, flip a few pages here, and look inside yourself for the answers to the new you.

1

Own Your Shit

Y'all, I get it. Ain't nothing easier than waiting for a fancy new, trauma-free you to swoop in and save you. I once waited for that, too. We say phrases like *New Year, New Me* or *Once I get a little bit of time or money,* then *I'm gonna make a move.* When we attach ourselves to these phrases, we're holding ourselves down in the mud rather than dusting our butts off and pushing on.

I'll let you in on a little tidbit: That kind of attitude got me nowhere. You know why? Because I was *choosing* to do nothing. I was *choosing* to let my hurt and trauma hold me down, rather than being active about making changes in the here and now.

But let's talk about you for a moment. You picked up this book because there's something you're unhappy with in your life. Might be one small thing, might be a lot of small things, or it might be one big thing. We all make excuses about why we are unhappy. I hear it all the time—"It's because I saw my mama or daddy raise me this way," or, "I saw them living that way..." As a child, there is often little that we can control. Our parents shape us and unfortunately they also traumatize us.

But.

But the minute you get agency over your life, it is *your* choice to continue that trauma, consciously or unconsciously. I ain't saying you can't assign some level of acknowledgment for where the trauma started, but *where it started* and *how it continues* are two different things. The most common example I see is in relationships. People write to me all the time, *MJ, you know, he's treating me like shit, and I don't know what to do, blah blah blah. Why do these kinds of men always choose me?* Honey, you asking the wrong questions! It ain't about him, it's about *you*. Why did *you* choose that person? Just because they chose you doesn't mean you gotta choose them back, you know. Just because you start with them doesn't mean you got to keep them around. *You're* the one choosing this life, and your life is a result of those choices.

Does that sting? It should.

It should make you think: *Yeah, I do this or that.* Now, does that action or behavior fall in line with the future you desire for yourself? Does it fall in line with the future you imagined? I guarantee you it does not. Because that behavior, that mindset, is a product of the concept I call "passive pain versus productive pain."

Most people operate with passive pain. Passive pain is the mindset of *it is what it is. I experienced such and such, or so-and-so happened to me that created pain in my life, and I am just passively experiencing it. This is just what my life is, I'm doing the best I can.* But really, you're doing nothing about it.

Sound familiar?

This just might be you now, but it doesn't have to be you in the future. That's where productive pain comes into play, the idea that *yes, I'm experiencing this pain, but I'm willing to experience a different kind of pain. The pain of change.* Productive pain is having an honest inventory of who you are. It means being able to say, *I don't like how my life is right now, whether it's in all areas or just this one area, and I don't like the pain I'm experiencing, so I'm willing to make a change.* And then *creating* that change because you don't wanna be out here all talk and no action, you know. Each of us has an idea of the future we desire, the person we want to be, and the level of life we want, and the first step in reaching that future, being that person, achieving that life is to let go of our current damaging self-image and to stop seeing ourselves through a filter of being "this or that." The future we desire for ourselves *requires* us to become not a different person, but an emotionally healed version of ourselves.

What does owning your shit look like? It could look like so many things, but it comes down to understanding and accepting that the level you desire to be on will *require* you to do something different. Maybe it means having to be more disciplined than you've ever been in the past, maybe it means having to focus harder than you've ever done, maybe it means cutting back on socializing. Maybe it means spending your finances a little differently because you need to save.

It might mean letting go of current relationships and some past patterns and making a conscious decision every day *not* to go looking for and choosing those same types of people. One of the things I had to do for myself was *own* the fact that I had been in some fucked-up past relationships. I couldn't blame them all on them being bad guys.

Because okay, did people hurt me in my past relationships?

Yeah.

But did I still *choose* those kinds of people repeatedly?

Yeah.

And did I inflict pain or damage on them, too? There's no way that I didn't. Even if I was protecting myself or just being me, there's no way I didn't *also* inflict pain upon them, too.

True healing and personal change mean being able to own that, yeah, you've made some bad choices, too. It's not just all someone else's fault. Being able to own that you are part of a dynamic, that's yin and yang—you're a part of every dynamic that has hurt you.

So, how do we go from passive pain to productive pain? Productive pain comes from sitting down with people that you've hurt—people who've told you that you hurt them and are willing to share how. Here's the hard part—first, you gotta sit down, shut the fuck up, and let them tell you. Even better: Ask them to write it down. Because sometimes you have to come in contact with pain in order to get over pain. Sit in the presence of those you've hurt and listen, actively listen, to them, and own up to yourself and your choices that have put you in this position.

Second, you have to *sit* in *your* pain. Without any numbing mechanisms. No alcohol, no weed—nothing that can be used as a crutch to shield you from or numb you to your own pain. Because, yeah, I see you. Ain't nothing new under the sun. I see your bottle, your drink, your blunt, that edible, or whatever you use to deaden away those feelings and numb yourself to avoid dealing with the real you. *Sit* in your pain and do nothing about it in that moment. Feel what you feel.

I feel horrible. I feel bad. I feel this. I feel that. Whatever you are feeling—sit in it.

I see your eyebrows rising, and I hear the question: *You just said passive pain was doing nothing. Now you want us to do nothing with our pain?* Productive pain requires a silent, still moment—it does *not* require a lifetime of stillness. Turning our passive pain into productive pain requires that we first *feel* that pain. That we muster up the strength to not run from it, to not hide from it, to not lie to ourselves about it. That's the very first step to reversing the complacency you've been feeling. Sitting in your pain *is* an active step because it takes mental strength to look your demons in the eye and face them without running. Because if you refuse to feel them feelings, you're never gonna be able to move on. Those feelings, they will resurface, and they will force you back to relying on those coping mechanisms. Anytime you're feeling stuck, taking the time to sit in your pain to process it, to understand it, to work through it, without numbing yourself or using an emotional or chemical crutch, is always the first step.

Sitting in your pain doesn't mean you always gotta be alone because believe me, that won't be the case 99 percent of the time. Life just doesn't work that way. Trigger moments, they're everywhere. Some you see coming, some you don't. But the key to productive pain is to recognize your trigger moment and *then* sit with it, with the pain, as it unfolds.

You *have* the tools already. It's just a matter of accepting that you have the tools and *using* them rather than waiting around for the New You to magically appear.

Using your tools, mind you, ain't like building a table. You aren't gonna be using your tools like that—no hammering, no drilling, nothing like that. In fact, the first step to get to where you want to be is to *let go*. Cut the dead weight. Think of it as removing that which did not serve you. For me, it was a matter of letting go of my trust issues, the shit that was holding me back professionally and personally. You can't get over that hurdle as long as you're holding on to the shit that holds you down. And the timing could not have been more perfect because just as I realized this, COVID hit, and it was actually very helpful in that it gave me a lot of time with myself. I did virtual therapy, which I've been doing for years, but I finally was able to really focus on it.

Therapy in general, not just during COVID, gave me the

opportunity to face myself in an unbiased environment. In therapy, your therapist didn't know you before you started, and, most likely, after you're done, this person's not gonna be your friend. There's that professional boundary there that offers you the environment you need to be able to fully open up and be transparent about who you are and what you're going through. The feedback you receive with that level of honesty is just invaluable.

For me, therapy's such a unique experience because when you're the head of the house, when you're the decision maker, when you're the one that everyone looks to, who's *your* sounding board? You may not always be comfortable sharing what you're going through with the people you're caring for, or even who you're in a relationship with, because maybe you don't wanna be vulnerable with them in that way just yet. Maybe you fear it'll make you seem weak to them. Maybe you fear it could be used against you in some capacity. So, for the strong ones out there, which I imagine many of you reading here are, therapy is a way to break through the isolation of your own baggage you're carrying so that you can have a sounding board to be able to process it into something more beautiful.

Therapy gave me the emotional tools to identify what I feel. So many people go through stuff, and they don't even know what *they* are really feeling about it. That's why we act out. That's why we shut down. That's why we yell. That's why we over-fuck. It's because we don't have the proper tools to process what we're going through. But therapy gives you the *language* to be able to communicate your feelings. It doesn't *change* your needs and feelings, but it does give you the language to be able to *communicate* your needs and feelings—to be able to say to your loved one, "You are really getting on my fucking nerves when you do this shit. How do we work through this?" It gives you the language to be able to say to yourself, "You know, I do like this, and I wanna explore myself more in this particular area." Therapy gave me these tools and the language to be able to communicate with myself and others about what's most important to me within my life.

Once my eye was fixed through the work I did in therapy, that was when things started changing, and for the better. I was able to take on a business partner. I hired business managers, accountants—the sky was the limit. I expanded my staff significantly—and who knew, but that actually meant *I* got to work less.

But the best thing that came out of that was the freedom I felt. Letting go of my trauma bonds—because some of our relationships, whether we want to admit it or not, are created from trauma. And when you let go of that, it *frees* you. It freed me to have better relationships. It freed me to become a better parent, brother, and son.

And it ain't about acquiring *new* tools. It's not about finding something you did not have.

It's about letting *go* of the things that color the way you view the world. Like taking off those lenses that filter your viewpoint. You ever wear a pair of sunglasses all day and take them off at the end of the day and see the sun for the first time? You think to yourself, *My God, this day is fucking beautiful!* It is *exactly* that. It is letting go of all that hurt and trauma and being able to see the world in its full light, and more importantly, see *yourself* in your full life, so that you can let go of those things that are keeping you from being able to experience life the way you deserve.

What it comes down to, for all of us, is our mentality and attitude. It comes down to whether or not we are able to look at ourselves and say, *my mentality, my attitude, is fucked-up.*

Nine times out of ten, it is. But it isn't always easy to recognize.

You ever been in one of those nice, high-end stores with them snooty staff members who do not want to give you the time of day because they are expecting you to spend nothing, so they treat you like nothing? I was in one with my nephew-son Marco, on Rodeo Drive, and this very thing happened. I've never been into designer clothes in any way, shape, or form. I couldn't afford those things for most of my life, so I just never developed an appreciation for them. First, it kept me from overspending, and second, I thought, *Why torture myself?* However, when my nephew-sons both came to live with me when they were seventeen, it was my introduction to parenting at a very unexpected time. When Marco and DJ moved to California, we didn't have a whole lot to do. I was in a very different place than I was years prior. Shopping was something that Marco liked to do, so that was something we would do together. And over time I started to realize, "Well, I kinda like nice shit, too." So, for me, this particular day happened to be one of those full-circle moments that you dream of being able to do as a kid, and that's why it was so disheartening when it turned into a really horrible experience. We walk in, and that feeling comes over me just like that.

So we walk up to this woman standing by the counter, and she is obviously meant to be helping customers. But because there isn't nobody but us in the whole place, there isn't nothing for her to do, so she's just standing there on her phone scrolling through TikTok. She does not even look up at us—and I know she heard us. My shoes got some sound to them. I *announce* myself, but to her it was like I was a goddamn invisible fly on the wall.

Well that lit a *fire* in me. So I step closer, and I draw myself up to my full height, and I don't mince my words. I make *sure* she hears me. I ain't shouting, but damn near close to it. And I say: "I would love for you to help me by giving your full attention, 'cause I'd like to spend money today and I need some assistance with that. Are you the person who is going to assist me or is someone else going to come out and do that for me?"

You *bet* she changed her tune just like that! Here's the thing I've always experienced: People will rise up to meet you at the level of expectations you place on them. So, if the expectation that I have of you is that you're gonna treat me like I'm subservient, like I'm less than, then you *will* treat me that way. However, if the expectation is *no, you need to rise on up and treat me with a certain level of respect,* then you're going to do that instinctively.

Although it was uncomfortable for me to initially go in on her, she eventually changed her behavior. Sometimes setting boundaries and forcing people to rise up is very uncomfortable for us because we're not accustomed to doing it. We're often taught directly and indirectly, especially women, *Don't make a fuss, don't be* that *Black woman or Black man.* We don't want to fit that stereotype of being aggressive. That means we often end up accepting a whole lot of disrespect outta trying to just get along. So, it's amazing when you set the expectation and communicate it very clearly. While you might feel uncomfortable because you may not be accustomed to doing that, that person will come up to meet you at that level. We ultimately ended up buying what we wanted, with that saleswoman's newfound attitude toward helping us.

I didn't think nothing of this behavior of mine at the time—it was just something I'd learned I needed to do to get my point across—but I understood the impact afterward when Marco said, "I want to be like that. You just go right for it and I admire that." When Marco said that to me, I suddenly felt like I was shrinking. Here was my nephew-son praising and admiring me, and all of a sudden I felt *smaller*—how does that work? It wasn't that my action was wrong; that woman was in the wrong, and if she had done her job from the start, there would have been no need for me to go off like that. But my attitude was not in the best place.

If I look at it from a purely intentional standpoint, then yes,

I was just fine. My intention (getting someone to help me) was clear, and the action (near cussing her out) got what I needed. My words got her act together, so mission accomplished, right? *Wrong.* I did not want to teach Marco that he should have that abrasive mentality to navigate the world in power.

I felt small because I realized there was another way I could have expressed the same point to that woman that was not so abrasive. I still did not have to be the abrasive person that I learned to be as the little gay boy growing up in the hood in the South. But those were tools I *learned* as that kid, which means I can now *unlearn* them because I don't need them anymore.

The funny thing is that once you let go of that defensive mentality, some of the rest snowballs with it. Once you realize *I don't need to act the same way I did growing up, I don't need to use those tools that way*, the same goes for how you live. Our past, our trauma, is reflected in the way we live. It perpetuates the self-abuse cycle; we live the way we did when we were getting hurt, consciously or subconsciously. The only way to get out of that is to consciously make the choice for the life you desire. You have to be *willing* to build your new self-image around that life rather than hold on to your self-image from the past.

Now, here's a pro tip for y'all who may be rolling your eyes at me and thinking, *I know I won't like it, whatever this new life is.* Okay, okay, I hear you. But just do this: Go for a drive. Drive to a beautiful open house of someone who has more than you. This isn't to knock you down but to open your eyes to what else is out there for you. Seeing, looking, witnessing—it tickles your senses, and if that can help you instill that conscious choice to change your life in some way, to *figure* a way out to improve your life, then I say all the better.

When I lived in this beautiful golf course community in the desert, I would go out at night and drive around the community. Then one day, I was driving through at like 11:00 a.m. and I see all these people standing about with their golf carts, some walking, just chitchatting the morning away. There were white and Black folks looking so prosperous. And I thought to myself, *Damn, we can all afford to be here, but they're enjoying their life when you're up all night. That* shifted my gears. That made me think, *I really need to change how I live my life. I need to change how I'm working.* And I knew there was a way—the evidence was right there in front of me at 11:00 a.m. on a fucking workday!

I ain't telling you to pack your shit up and move. You can be perfectly happy with your life—content and fulfilled—and *still* acknowledge there are better ways to exist. Because once you do, you become open to trying new things because there ain't no way to get better or experience better without first understanding this. So, instead of thinking there's a New Me out there, look at it this way. You have an idea of who you want to become. Your future you. The *better* you. All you gotta do is own your shit. And that's the scariest thing in the world because it begins and ends with looking at yourself.

Let's say that you're visiting family over the holidays. You know, this happens a lot during the holidays; happiest time of the year, no shit. So, you're visiting and then that one person comes in that you just don't fuck with and says that one thing that just triggers you. And those feelings that follow the triggers probably aren't very comfortable. They produce a hyper-temperamental response, a feeling that we need to *do* something about it. We think we need to numb it away. Scream it away. Fuck it away. Drink it away.

Don't do that.

Let yourself feel what you feel because the pain that we're afraid of experiencing is exactly what's keeping us away from the power that we're going to need in order to grow. You have to allow yourself to truly grieve the impact of the choices you made within your life so that you can then heal from it. Whatever your brain is screaming at you to do, ignore it. Sitting in our pain is a choice. A choice to not do what we would normally do. So, if you normally snap back, don't. If you normally smoke it up, don't. If you normally get drunk, don't. Whatever your itch is, don't scratch it. Don't feed it. It may feel great in the moment to fall back on your normal response and let your temper manifest, but if you get up in their face, you're gonna be super animated. You're riled up, feeling triggered, coming at them real aggressive. How are they gonna respond to you? In kind. Now *you've* triggered *them,* and it all repeats. Every single time. And now you've become a part of the very dynamic that hurts you.

So just sit.

Yes, it will be uncomfortable. Even painful. It will make you fidget and cry and shout and scream on the inside. But you know what? Let it happen. It needs to happen. You need this in order to grow, in order to take charge of yourself, your future, and become the person you want to become. So don't get shy on me now, don't you dare.

Let your heart race. *I need to tell so-and-so this, I'm gonna do that*... no, sir, none of that. Let yourself cry. Let yourself be pissed the fuck off. Let yourself feel what it feels like to be triggered because you *know* your normal response does not serve you—you know that. You *know* that your current tool kit is not effective. Take a deep breath, feel what you gotta feel, and then get up and leave. If you're at a relative's house in the dining room or wherever else, get out of that room and go elsewhere. The hall, the backyard, the living room, even the bathroom. Go sit on the toilet, pants down if it helps. The important thing is you need to get away from the thing that's triggering you.

Now you're alone, in whatever space you've carved out for yourself, and the emotions, the feelings, they're coming down. Maybe not all at once, but little by little. Your heart slows. Your palms dry up. You feel the high coming down. If it's possible—and I'm bankin' it is because everyone keeps their phone on them—write it down. Just write down what you're feeling. Get out of your mind. If you've got a piece of paper, the back of an envelope, a scrap of napkin, and a pen, even better because you can't erase it.

And this ain't the time to get pretty with your words—in fact, get ugly. Stream of thought, no periods, no commas, no nothing but how you feel. Write out everything you're feeling in this moment. Don't bottle it up. Let it flush its way out of your mind by writing it down. Let it *shrink* in significance by putting pen to paper because sometimes, you'll realize it's maybe not as bad as you thought once you see it written out in front of you. Maybe you'll see that it was more mental than anything. It may even help you to empathize with the person who triggered you—not agree, maybe, but empathize. You think you would've empathized with them if you'd reacted like you normally do? Hell no.

Sitting in our pain allows us to feel the discomfort, and what happens is we start to become desensitized to such triggers. We realize that discomfort is not all that uncomfortable. And what you'll also begin to realize is that the discomfort of sitting in your pain and that triggering moment without trying to do anything about it—*that* pain—is far less than the pain and the discomfort that results when you do react with your typical response.

If you snap back, you perpetuate the never-ending cycle of triggers, and you deal with the pain of that. If you fuck it away and fuck someone you ain't got no business fucking, you'll deal with the regret. If you drink too much and end up making some poor decisions, you'll deal with the guilt. And it's much, *much* harder for that type of pain—the pain that comes from making multiple bad choices after being triggered—to leave you alone. So you end up realizing that the passive pain is often far greater than the productive pain of just sitting with it. That productive pain will dissipate, with no struggle or push, and you will be left with the freedom to put it all behind you and move forward because it has nothing to do with who you are today and who you can become.

Your past has no place in your future. So don't let your trauma, your shit, your baggage, have a front-row seat in designing who you are. Own your shit, and then change your shit.

Take Action to Get the F*ck Out Your Own Way

The next time you get triggered, and I don't care where it is or who you're with, deal with that pain productively. Check in with yourself and ask yourself, *How would I normally respond?* Then ask yourself, *Does that response hurt me?*

And whatever that reaction is, don't do it.

Sit with it and feel.

Remove yourself from your trigger.

If you can, write out what you feel. But most importantly, just allow yourself to be uncomfortable.

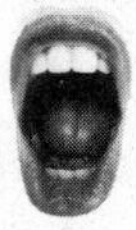

2

Change Your Shit

Some of our trauma comes from our parents, there ain't no way around it. And they don't have to be divorced or show any of those outward signs of distress to have traumatized you, either. That's not how generational trauma works. It's in the little things, though they may not feel little when they're happening. But the small stuff—what they say and do—acts in our triggering moments. And more likely than not, it's how *you* do some of the same things now that you're in their shoes.

I can hear you shouting, *I am not my parents!*

You may not be, but let me tell you this: Trauma is handed down. From your great-great-great-grandparents all the way down to you. And for Black people in *particular*, because of our history of long-standing bondage in America, we have a unique relationship with ancestral trauma. Four hundred years ago, our ancestors were brought to North America in chains, and four hundred years of generations of Black people have stemmed from that. From the first days our ancestors stepped onto these shores, bound in shackles and chains, they were treated as subhuman. That mentality, that persisting treatment and degradation, has had inevitable lasting effects on our race and in our culture. We began to see *ourselves* that way, through the lens of those in power. And that viewpoint, that lens that was forced upon us, was handed down between families for generations. Slavery mentality did not stop with the Civil War and the Emancipation Proclamation; it runs far and deep in every Black family, this mindset that the abuse and suffering from our history is the standard way we live.

This generational trauma has become a disease from which we all suffer. It comes out in every aspect of our lives. It comes out in our relationships with family, with friends, and with partners. It comes out in power dynamics, most often seen in how we view parenting as some sort of hierarchical relationship, a dictatorship, if you will. *That* is the echo of slave mentality still ringing hard and true today. That is the remnants of the shit we learn, of us taking slave mentality and applying it to the relationships we have. It's in the *it's my way or the highway, I'm the Father, Son, and the Holy Ghost, so, motherfucker, you gonna listen to me* way that people may treat their kids. It comes out verbally, physically, passively, nonverbally, and all of the above—there are no bounds to how this generational trauma can show up in our lives and get handed down to our kids. That's what makes it so difficult to pinpoint. It could come from anywhere, any aspect of our lives, but all this generational trauma stems from that deep racial oppression that still runs through our country.

When we look at ourselves as individuals—and look back at our parents and generations before us—we can see that this generational trauma handed down by a slave mentality comes out in the suppression of our feelings. It comes out in our lives and experiences in the trauma our parents experienced, in the triggers our parents picked up and passed on to us. In the South, particularly, that was the culture. The way of life. I didn't grow up in a culture where people were encouraged or expected to tell you how they felt, to talk to you about anything other than the business at hand. Keep your business to yourself and don't involve nobody else. It ain't their concern. And you know, that can be good for some things, but not for solving generational trauma.

My parents, they didn't grow up with any idea of how to solve their own trauma or understand their own triggers. So what I got was merely the outcome of when I triggered them. A good example of this in my household was how silence was used to prove a point. In the South, it wasn't the culture for parents to apologize to their kids. And if they did, it wasn't a real apology. It might have *sounded* like a quick apology, but it was really them blaming me for making them react the way they did because if

I hadn't done that thing, they wouldn't have reacted that way. It was a quick, "I'm sorry," and that's it. Never apologizing for what they did specifically, never offering an explanation for their actions or nothing. And more often than not, I didn't even get those words. All I got was silence.

That punishment of the silent treatment was one of the worst things I experienced as a child. I tell you. I hated it. Absolutely *hated* it. It traumatizes kids because it makes them believe that the only way to be seen and feel like they are enough is to make other people happy. What it does is it teaches children to not say their real opinions, to not be a whole person out of fear of upsetting others. *Gee, I don't wanna lose you* type of mentality. *I don't want you to ignore me.* It plays on people's abandonment issues—actually, it's often what *creates* people's abandonment issues. This behavior plays on people's fear of rejection. This form of abuse is called *stonewalling*. It doesn't do anything but hurt your relationship with whoever you're doing it to. For me, when I was a child, it hurt my relationship with my parents.

This Black generational trauma also comes in the form of broken families when one parent or both start vilifying the other. A mother might say, "Your father hurt me in this way, he taught me this, he did this to me, so I figure I'll be that way to you." A father may say, "I can't stand your mama now. She put me through so much shit, and I'm gonna take that out on you by not coming around, by abandoning you." Our parents might think or rationalize it to themselves that they're protecting us from the way *they* were treated, but in doing so, they don't realize that they are *unintentionally* perpetrating that hurt and trauma *onto* you.

So what if y'all had fucked-up dynamics? Okay, so you did. Own that. But we gotta ask ourselves, *Just because I don't like my child's father or my child's mother, are they treating the* child *that way?* Is there evidence of the other parent treating the kid in the way that you perceive they've treated you? And be honest. If it's a no, then that kid's gotta have a relationship with both parents. Because y'all are grown and need to learn to handle your shit without depriving your child of a healthy relationship with their other parent.

Demonizing each other is only gonna cause problems down the road when the child is old enough to wonder why they didn't have a relationship with that other parent. And when they do, I guarantee you, they will not give a good god*damn* about *your* reasons. They're gonna resent the fuck out of you, and more power to them. Because they did not ask for you to take your anger and hurt out on them—all they wanted was to know both their parents, and that was taken away from them without their say. They will be old enough to think and say, "You know what? He, she, they, was bad to you. To *you.* But you, you are doing the same to *me* trying to protect me." That resentment is gonna be taken out, in one way, shape, or form, and that payment will come due—be it in the form of damage to the actual relationship with the child or the loss of their trust down the road.

Weaponizing kids is yet another way this generational trauma is handed down from generation to generation, as some of you may know. Holding kids ransom, saying, *If you don't do this, you cannot see them. If you don't pay this, you cannot see them.* Using a child as a tool to hurt somebody else. And no one likes being used.

Once a child is old enough to recognize they're being used or have been used, it's gonna come back around and bite that parent in the ass. Hard. Because that day *will* come when the child is old enough to understand what's happening around them. And when they do—not *if* but when—it's gonna damage the relationship.

So many folks, they write to me, saying, *I'm not gonna let so-and-so see their kid and blah blah blah. And, MJ, you'll be so proud of me because I'm not letting them see such-and-such, until they XYZ.* Like it's a *virtuous* thing they're doing!

Oh no, I ain't proud. I'm *afraid.* Because those kids are gonna grow up hating—or, at the very least, resenting—that parent one day. If this one-sided story is fed to them, they will realize sooner or later that there is a dissonance. They will realize there are lies planted there, that this whole concept of weaponization is based on some level of dishonesty. Or at the very least that they ain't getting the full picture. That they aren't able to see all the perspectives. They will get old enough to recognize for themselves that "he or she or they wasn't bad. They may have been bad to you, but they weren't bad to me."

What's more, this dissonance they've been fed will lead them to seeing that neither parent is perfect—and it was alright that they wanted to spend time with both imperfect parents. But they couldn't. So, why're you acting surprised when the child's thirteen or fourteen and they don't trust you when you've been lying about core shit their whole life? Ain't it no wonder they don't want your guidance now? It's the price you pay. A very heavy price that goes far beyond the gratification of hurting the other parent.

Generational trauma also plays out in the form of blaming kids for the way *we* are, for making them feel like us parenting them means we deserve a damn reward. Raise your hand if you've ever heard a parent say, "You piss me off. You make me mad because if it wasn't for you doing this, if I didn't have to come up to your school every day..." or any variation of those lines. Blaming them for your moods, for your reactions, that's a big one.

I wouldn't react if it wasn't for you, I'm gonna beat all y'all's asses, you're the reason I have no self-control, blah blah blah.

Really?

Okay, let's go with that. That is toxic, traumatizing behavior. You're teaching kids that the only way to be loved is by doing things, that they are responsible for *your* behavior. That's a horrible thing to teach. It perpetuates abuse. It perpetuates self-blame. In the long run, it teaches kids—who then become traumatized adults—that they must pander to someone else's moods in order to be loved, that they are *worthy of abuse* if they don't do exactly as those they seek love from tell them to.

I see it everywhere, in so many places, from so many people—I *was* one of those people with this lesson I had to unlearn. You know how many people are out there sitting in abusive relationships, getting their ass beat emotionally, physically, financially, and blaming *themselves* for it?

They say shit like this to a friend, to a therapist: *"I want to become a better XYZ; I wanna be better because I make him, her, them, so upset. I do this and I do that, and they get so angry, they do this and that back."*

Well, guess what? *That ain't your fault!* Maybe you did something the way your partner didn't want. Maybe you triggered them. But—and say it with me—*you are not responsible for their responses.*

Who is responsible for their responses?

They are.

They are, and no one else. It's *their* issue if they respond in a vicious manner. And that's one of the hardest things to unlearn, to let go of that responsibility, because we've been taught it by so many people from childhood. We've been taught to engage with the world and other people that way through our passed-down generational trauma, that we are responsible for other people's feelings and their reactions when we really aren't.

So, how can we change our shit when the trauma of our past still reverberates in our everyday lives? One of the ways that

I have been able to recognize and work through my trauma comes not just from myself, but through my kids. I expected to become a parent through adoption or through some other, quote, unquote, more traditional means. But it has always been a very endearing experience for me. Challenging because I don't know anyone, regardless of how you come into parenting, who would say it's *easy*. I would say that it's the hardest job on earth. But one of the things that parenting has taught me has been to be compassionate toward other people's processes in terms of where they're at. It has taught me to set and keep very clear boundaries. 'Cause if you do not have boundaries with your children, get ready for some real fuck shit to evolve. Believe it or not, it has made me a better dater. 'Cause when you're dating, you don't want to have just *anyone* around your kids. I made a lot of really bad dating choices until I became a parent. Parenting gives you another source of accountability to say, "Do I really wanna bring this motherfucker around my kids? Do I really want my boys to see me dealing with this, accepting that?" It's a different level of accountability for how you treat yourself and how you allow other people to treat you.

But for all you parents out there, you know that we've all had those moments when parenting made us reengage our trauma because our kids—oh my *God*, they're with us *all* the time. They know us inside and out. They call us out. They try us in ways we would *never* have dared with our own parents.

They are our mirrors. They force us to see ourselves and how others see us and how they respond to us. And if we're not paying close attention, we will blame them; we will say their responses to us are their fault without seeing how we contribute to them. But that's the beauty of parenting: It *forces* us to see who we are all the time because we can't just turn it on and off.

Pro tip for y'all: Don't box yourself in or try to pretend you're something you're not. Be open about the things that have traumatized you, whether with your kids, your partner, or your friends. Give them the chance to see you as a human being, number one, by letting them humanize you. Tell them who you are and what you've been through, even if you need to tell your story age-appropriately, you know. Let's be real, don't go telling a two-year-old your entire abuse story start to finish, but that doesn't mean you can't come down to their level and humanize yourself to them.

I grew up in a home and a culture where your parents, or any adult for that matter, did not apologize to you. No matter how wrong they were, you ain't getting an apology. They just brushed it off, and you were expected to do the same. So I grew up not really knowing *how* to apologize, sincerely and humbly and without anything else attached. I did not know how to do that, not until my kids started calling me out. Because when they did, I had this moment—this eye-opening, painfully intrinsic moment—where I realized I'd fucked up. And if I wasn't careful, I was gonna re-traumatize my kids in the same way.

My nephew-son Marco and I were in Florida, and we'd been

out for a little while on the road. It was a long day, a hot day. I had one of my business partners with me, and I was filming the whole time. I was also in a really shitty mood. Something kept going wrong off camera, I can't even remember what it was, but whatever it was, it kept me on camera for way too long. I could not *wait* to get off-screen and just be done with the day. But everyone around us didn't seem to see the problem.

The minute I get off camera, I just lose it. I am cussing *everyone* out: "Is no one gonna do this? And why the fuck am I on camera?" Then I pause, and I realize my phone is nowhere to be seen, and the next thing that comes out of my mouth is "Where the *fuck* is my phone?"

Now, that was just the damn icing on the cake. Next thing you know, everyone is scrambling to find my phone. And I'm just standing there that whole time saying shit, and before I know it, Marco's at my shoulder looking at me, saying *I* could look harder. Because I ain't doing nothing; I'm just barking at everyone else. So, I go off on him, too, and, you know what? He just keeps on looking at me. Then he hands me my phone. I take it and just leave. He follows me on the elevator to go downstairs. The minute those doors close, he says, "You can't talk to me like that."

I swear, my head turned like in *The Exorcist*. I went, "Excuse me?" and Marco pulled his tone together and went: "I don't appreciate when you talk to me like that. You were in a bad mood and you taking it out on me. And I don't like when you take your mood out on me. I'm here to help you. I ain't done nothing wrong with you. You shouldn't do that."

I *wish* I could say I handled it all graceful and adultlike and shit, but true to form, my dramatic ass took over. I hit some random button and just walked off the elevator because I felt *confronted.* I felt like I could do nothing, so I walked off wearing these victim tears, when I hadn't been the victim of *anything* at this point! But that was my traumatized reaction speaking. As I walked down the hallway sniffling back tears that didn't even make sense, it occurred to me, maybe God's voice or somewhere from above, saying, "You're an asshole. You need to apologize."

So I go downstairs, and I see Marco right away—he's sitting by the pool, and he's sitting there hunched over. He looks so sad and hurt.

I walk right up to him and I say, "I'm so sorry. I didn't mean to hurt your feelings."

He looks up at me, and his expression hit me then and there. *I was traumatizing him. He didn't deserve to have to carry my own shit.*

So I sat down and said, "You have nothing to apologize for. I give you permission to be honest about how you experience me because I'm just so used to being me, like we all are, that sometimes I just don't see it. I don't know how I impact other people sometimes unless they show me, and that doesn't mean that I haven't dipped from paying attention to my own behavior, but I give you permission to tell me about myself because it may be some blind spot that I can't see, but you can."

I clearly had not dealt with this situation as calmly as I could have. But in this moment, I sat him down, and I told him that from a young age, as a little gay Black boy growing up in the South, I learned to navigate life by being direct. In some cases that meant using anger as a way to get people's attention and get them to do what I wanted, and at the same time, keep them from hurting me. I did that my whole childhood, so that behavior, it's *ingrained* in me. I have to *unlearn* that shit. I'm no good at knowing how to control my anger. So he knows that I'm trying, that I don't always know how to stop or when I should stop, and that he always has permission to tell me that I'm doing it again.

That honesty about who I am as a human being and that this is hard for me helps in giving kids a level of empathy toward you. It creates a softening vulnerability because people are gonna see you as a human rather than as a behavioral pattern—and let me tell you: We *love* to define our behavior patterns rather than define ourselves as a human being who just feels things and is triggered in different ways.

But defining those patterns creates shame. *Take* that shame away from you. Remember: Sharing your story ain't anything to be ashamed of. Do what you need to do and be transparent. Doesn't matter if your kid is seven or twenty-seven; have that conversation. If you're feeling off, feeling bad, explain it.

"You know, sometimes Mommy feels very heavy. Mommy feels. You know how you feel a little testy sometimes? Sometimes Mommy feels testy, and Mommy don't want to put that on you."

The same conversation can be had if you're a father, older sibling, auntie, or uncle—you can and should have this conversation with anyone of a younger generation, anyone who you have authority or power over. Just put it out there. It creates such a beautiful, vulnerable relationship, and it knocks *down* that slave mentality we got that parenting is a dictatorship rather than a relationship. Knocking that mentality down will serve both parties in the long run.

So much of this generational trauma we talked about in the beginning of the chapter deals with how parents burn bridges with their children, but having an open and honest conversation does just the opposite. As kids get older, we realize that the most beautiful thing is the bond we have with them and the trust they have in telling us anything and knowing that when they leave the house, they will still want to have a relationship with you, that they'll be *itching* to talk to you because they see you as someone they connect with. They understand the authority you have of being a parent, but they know that first and foremost you love them.

My wake-up call with Marco allowed me to really see *myself* in the way Marco saw me, which helped me realize that I was not teaching him how to deal with trauma in a way that was beneficial. I had to give him permission to tell me how he truly experienced me. I had to be willing to apologize to him when he told me I was hurting him. That has been *tremendously* helpful in both working through my *own* trauma and teaching my kids how to get through theirs. But the key to doing all of that is your will to accept the fact that you *are* traumatized in the first place.

There are three phases to change. The first phase is to **own your shit**. You have to be real and say to yourself, *Oh my God, I do that shit. I just did that shit this morning!* We've all been there, so don't run from that feeling. Sit in that pain, but don't beat yourself up because that ain't gonna make anything better. Now you know better, so you can do better. You did the best you could then, which, in all likelihood, was what you experienced yourself growing up. That's what generational trauma does. It's handed-down trauma that we just repeat over and over again to ourselves and to the next generation. But now that we know that, we can move forward.

Being able to recognize what you're doing while you're doing it does *not* mean always stopping, because I'll tell you right now, in this phase, in the very beginning, you're not going to always be able to stop yourself.

Should you try? Absolutely. But you won't always succeed.

In fact, you might sometimes end up doing it even *worse*, and that's gonna be a bitter pill to swallow. The key is to respond by not looking at the person who just triggered you like, *This fucking crazy bitch, who do they think they are?* If you do—and I know because I've done this more times than I care to count—they will look right back at you and get just as defensive, like, *Why you looking at me like that?* That kind of mentality is only gonna prompt an abrasive response, and before you know it, it's like, *Oh God, I'm doing it again.* Cycle repeats.

Second, you have to be willing to **recognize what you do when you're triggered**. Then you can make a conscious choice to do something different. It is *not* about learning to not be triggered. It's about learning what your triggers are and how to recognize them, so you can make another choice. You may be triggered your whole life. You can spend twenty, thirty, forty, fifty, sixty years reinforcing this triggering behavior, and that shit is never gonna go away. But you can make an alternative choice at that point in time. Like the example I gave before, talking to your own children—or any member of the next generation—in an age-appropriate way to explain to them what your challenge is.

The third and final stage of change is to **make the choice to show love**. I grew up with the silent treatment punishment. Whenever I did something wrong, whenever I made my parents upset, they would just shut down. And you know what happened? I became *fearful*. I felt like I was not enough, for them, for anyone. Treating someone with silence sends them toward all these negative emotions, which defeats the very purpose that you're trying to use your anger to achieve. You want them to see the point? Love, not silence, is the easiest way to get them there. People don't feel loved in silence. They feel abandoned. They feel scared.

Here's the thing: It's not about whether or not the child can see how upset you are. It's about them seeing that they're loved in that moment. It's about them receiving that love no matter how upset you are. When people see and feel that, it generally makes them more responsive and receptive to hearing and processing the thoughts about what they might have done that was upsetting to you. Once they feel loved, *then* you can have that discussion with them. But not before, because if the child is operating from a place of fear, of abandonment, then they ain't gonna receive what you have to say.

We are less likely to traumatize our kids when we humanize them and ourselves. When we empathize with them. *Why did they do what they did? They didn't do this shit to piss us off.* It's not about excusing poor choices; it's about empathizing with why that choice might have been made in the first place, shifting our minds to think that perhaps this will throw open the gates for an honest and productive conversation between you and whoever it might be you're having this moment with.

Whether you are a parent or not, you gotta understand where your pain and trauma come from. It's deep, it's generational, it's damn difficult to own and change. But you gotta know, you gotta understand that *you* are the source of your problems, yes, but you are *also* the source of every solution. Own it. Don't beat anyone down; don't make anyone feel ashamed. Remind them of their power, and they will remind you of yours. It's amazing how much we can do when we realize that *we* have the power to do it.

Take Action to Get the F*ck Out Your Own Way

Now that we understand where our shit, our trauma, is coming from, ask yourself these questions:

How was I parented?

What parts of being parented did I like, did I dislike? And none of that "oh, my mama, my papa, they did the best they could." Take them off those pedestals. You know they did their best, but what pissed you off? What did they do, specifically?

And once you've answered those questions, here's the kicker: What, of any of those things you just mentioned, might you be doing today? They might look different, they might not come across in the same way, but guaranteed, some of that shit trickled down to you. You just gotta realize it and make that effort to change.

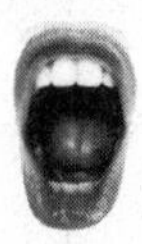

3

Stop People Pleasing and Know Your Worth

Self-worth is one of the *nastiest* of life's clusterfucks to untangle, which of course means it is gonna be one of the *first* we have to deal with. We are living in a time when too many folks do not know their own worth because they've gotten used to the world telling them they don't have any. We think our own self ain't something worth caring for. If you don't know your worth, then all you're doing is opening yourself up to so many different avenues to be hurt. One of the ways I often see this manifested is in becoming a people pleaser as a way to compensate for our own lack of self-worth.

People pleasing is the act of bending to the will and needs of others, even if we don't want to, because we fear their disapproval if we don't. And this shit goes hand in hand with a lack of self-worth, because in order for me to always say yes to others, that means I gotta say no to *myself* in critical times when I *need* to be saying yes to *myself* instead. When we live with a habit of people pleasing, we are *denying* ourselves access to our needs, wants, and desires just to make *someone else* happy. *That's* self-abuse. These habits come from a miserable place within us where we have very poorly defined self-worth, self-esteem, and worthiness. Yes, you know it. Don't be shaking your head at me, because I know I am spitting truths. So listen up: No matter who the people are that you're trying to please, you need to know that people pleasing is about *not* knowing your worth, and it *is* a form of self-abuse; let's just be clear about that.

Here's how it works: When you feel like you're not enough, in any aspect of your life, that is a *self-worth* issue, which leads to a lack of boundaries and ultimately culminates in people-pleasing behavior. Think of your boundaries as your house. As you learn to *set* boundaries, that house becomes bigger. It becomes a mansion. It lets you live in luxury because having boundaries is akin to living the life *you* want.

Boundaries provide you with freedom, joy, and *protection* from all the fuck shit. But the bigger the mansion, the bigger the *foundation* needed to support it. You cannot put a mansion on anything other than a rock-solid foundation. Imagine what your home would look like built on top of a flimsy foundation. If that foundation is insecure, then your boundaries don't have a chance of staying up when someone or something comes knocking. That foundation is your self-worth, and if you don't have a healthy self-worth to *maintain* your boundaries, then there's a whole lot of people who are not going to treat you right until you fucking do it yourself. With no boundaries—or boundaries barely there because of shaky self-esteem—our old friend the people pleaser comes into play.

Most of us learned to people please early in life. I know I did. And it's a habit that has followed me throughout my life and really fucked me up in a lot of ways. It fucked me up in my relationships when I refused to speak up after seeing red flags because I still wanted whoever I was dating at the time to like me. It fucked me up when I didn't end relationships—with friends, with romantic partners, or with family—because I was more concerned about how it would hurt *their* feelings than concerned for myself over having an unhealthy relationship that didn't serve me. In all these situations I'd fill that gap in the relationship with people pleasing rather than focusing on how I wasn't getting what *I* needed from the relationship.

What truly fucked me up was giving people more than they deserved and not holding them accountable when they didn't meet my needs. It cost me *money*. It cost me *time*. It *definitely* cost me a lot of heartache. All the while, I convinced myself that I wasn't a people pleaser so much as I was a nice person. I let people pleasing happen for too long in my life until I realized that it *wasn't* that I was so giving to other people because I was a nice person. Because how the *fuck* are you going to be a "nice" person when you're not being nice to yourself? No, I wasn't "nice." I was an abusive person abusing myself.

I'm betting many of you feel this way.

So, how do we get from people pleasing to pleasing ourselves? That's a question I've heard so many times and from so many people across the board, but for many of us it's a hard one to tackle because once we ask ourselves that question, we don't know where to go from there. The very act of being a people pleaser is all bound up with shame, making it a scary place inside of us to explore. Once we realize that we're people pleasing and serving those who aren't serving us, we might very well try to put a stop to that shit—only to realize that it's now become a habit that we're shocked as hell to find we can't simply break. That's where the shame comes in. We feel ashamed that we are abusing ourselves, ashamed that we let people use us. And that shame holds us in place, stuck as fuck; we're making no moves to change our behavior to healthier patterns that serve *us* rather than *them*. But here's the thing: You can't *change* what you're too busy feeling ashamed of. The only way to change it is to remove that shame and see the root of all of this. Just as it was for owning your shit and changing your shit, we first gotta explore the root of where all this shit comes from in order to understand how to change it in our lives moving forward.

My journey to stop people pleasing never even got started until I recognized what the root of my people pleasing was, which was the *unresolved trauma* that made me *believe* that the only safety in this world was to make other people happy. First, I had to get to the root of my unresolved trauma and work through it. And that's what you're gonna have to do, too.

There is always a *reason* for our behavior. People pleasing ain't no exception. I guarantee you that there was some moment or event in your life that made you feel that *this*—making others happy at the cost of your own happiness—was the *right* thing to do. When people come to me with this issue, I ask them, "What is the earliest memory in your life of being a people pleaser?" Maybe it was dealing with an emotionally unstable parent or a guardian figure who had an addiction. A lot of the time it does root back to our parental units or people in our early lives who were unstable or abusive in some way, shape, or form, and your safety was only guaranteed in making them happy.

For me, the act of people pleasing got me through my childhood years. It had a purpose. It had a *reason* to exist. Let me paint y'all a picture. Imagine growing up in the South, in the *hood*, as a little gay Black boy. I've always been tiny, but back then I was *really* tiny. And back then I was like, *I'll beat your ass with a damn bat or whatever I can grab, but I don't wanna go to jail.* I knew that I would be seen as a mark out in the world. So I had to come up with something, or I was gonna get my ass beat every day in school.

You know how the teachers and student body like to give out superlatives, like "most popular" or "best dressed"? I remember *distinctly* that I never got "best dressed" because we didn't have much money. I never got "most popular" because I was introverted and afraid of people. But here's what I *did* get: I *always* got the title of *nicest person*. And for the longest time, I thought of that as a compliment. But what I realized was that being called the nicest all the time wasn't exactly a compliment. Nor was it my intention to be *liked*. My whole reason for being nice was to be *safe*. My mode of protecting myself was through people pleasing. Being friendly, being the nice guy, was my protection. It played a *huge* part in getting me through school. It allowed me to walk down the hallways and not have people try to jump me because I was gay. When someone did try to pick on me, it allowed other kids to feel sympathetic and step in and say, "He's nice. Leave him alone."

As I told y'all before, the silent treatment was used in my home when I was kid, and that shit fucked me up and molded me into a people pleaser probably worse than anything else did. It traumatized the shit outta me and made me believe that the only way to be seen and loved and valued was to make other people happy so that they would not ignore me. This silent treatment most likely *created* my abandonment issues, which often go hand in hand with people-pleasing behavior within us. People pleasing became a defense mechanism, and a good one, even as I didn't yet realize that it was so unhealthy. It worked. I just didn't throw out the habit when its expiration date rolled around. It's like old milk sitting in the refrigerator: When I *bought* it, this shit was worth drinking. But now it's not, and I just didn't realize I needed to throw this habit out. And that moment when you can finally throw it out is so freeing.

That's what we have to recognize about people pleasing: the expressions of our trauma within our adult life *are* often rooted in some very *practical utility* from when we were younger. So, once you can identify that early memory in *your* life, then you can recognize that while your people pleasing may not serve you *now*, that doesn't mean it didn't serve you at some point in time. Knowing that fact makes it a hell of a lot easier to forgive ourselves for being people pleasers when we understand how our circumstances demanded it. Knowing this lifts that veil of shame because people pleasing doesn't own you anymore. *You* own *it*. *You* acknowledge *it*, and *you* can *change* it.

Once you've done the work of taking away that guilt and shame, then you can move on to dealing with your current people-pleasing behavior, the last bits of milk that you haven't yet thrown out. Remember: It served a purpose once upon a time, but that time is over now. It's expired. It doesn't work like it used to because *you* have changed. You're not that person anymore who needed people pleasing for protection, just like I'm not that scared little boy who used to walk down the hallways hoping no one would notice me. Now I'm a grown man standing before a camera in front of millions of people on any given day—everyone's watching me.

Now, don't get me wrong—I understand that old habits

die hard, and it can feel almost impossible to just kick a long-held habit cold turkey. Once you've gone back to the root and stripped away the guilt and shame, you might see that you are *still* people pleasing because you can't just flip a switch and banish it forever. But what you *can* do is not let people pleasing rule over you silently anymore. To this end, there are what I like to call "house rules" for people pleasing—because as y'all know, I still struggle with this shit day in and day out, too. Ain't no way you can do something for as long as I have and expect that it's going to magically turn around just because you read a book or watched a YouTube video. But we can recognize that that milk has gone sour and we can toss it out bit by bit until it's all gone.

What it really comes down to is allowing yourself to step *beyond* the shame that keeps you silent about it. That's why we go back to the beginning, so don't you even think about skipping this step. We are truly our own worst critics, and if you don't believe that and you are a people pleaser, well, you've got it backward. There ain't nothing more critical than abusing yourself because you want to make others happy and thinking you're so far below that you don't matter. But here's a little secret: When you can identify where it started, what you are also often able to identify is that at the time it was necessary and a utility.

But when this people-pleasing behavior goes unchecked, so grows the pile of unexpressed nos we say to ourselves. They might seem harmless at first. It's just another no, another thing you deny yourself. But eventually that shit becomes passive-aggressiveness. It shows up as those nice-nasty folks. Those people who, on the surface, *appear* like they're being nice, but underneath they're full of anger and resentment. Passive-aggressiveness is just the byproduct of all those unexpressed nos. And just like any other emotion or thought that keeps getting shoved under or buried farther down so that we don't have to deal with it, these nos *will* come to light—often in unpredictable, explosive ways.

I *know* you know what I'm saying. Ain't no way you, if you're a people pleaser, have escaped this scenario, because it *always* happens. Like fuckin' clockwork. Like a fuckin' ticking time bomb. It *will* go off.

Our anger and resentment of others—even of the world—build up over time. We ain't angry motherfuckers out here looking to cuss out the woman at Starbucks just because she didn't make our coffee right. We're not screaming at our partners when they do something we don't like just because we feel like it. What's happening in these moments is that we *are* struggling to communicate our needs. What happens every time, *every time*, you say yes when you want to say no is that unexpressed no gets sent to your internal *pressure cooker*. And then, at some point in time, it comes out in the form of rage or anger. Now it's six months later and it's built up, it's had all this time in the world to cook and pressurize, and suddenly you find yourself cussing someone the fuck out and throwing their clothes out the window. Yes, I *have* done that. That's how I know.

That's how I know that the no we're so afraid of expressing *always* becomes a buildup. And that buildup will end up expressing itself in the form of a *larger* blowup later on. *Always.* You will pay the consequences for being a people pleaser, there's no way around it. And the next thing you know, you look like the asshole! They'll be like, *Oh, she got such a bad attitude. You need to de-stress. There's something wrong with you.* And you might be sitting here thinking, *I've been like this the whole time, you should have read that shit and knew what was up with me.* Well, no. They don't know how to read that shit. They just think you're a bitch.

That's why we need to learn to express ourselves earlier. That's why we need to check into our self-worth and rebuild that foundation so we can hold on to our boundaries and nip that awful people pleasing in the bud. If you had *had* the courage and willingness to simply say no when you wanted to say no in the first place, you wouldn't have *had* to get to the point of being passive-aggressive. You wouldn't have *had* such an explosion of anger, nor would whatever relationship or friendship affected have been hurt to the same degree. If you had *had* a greater sense of self-worth, you would have had stronger boundaries in your arsenal. Boundaries that would have *allowed* you to say no. Boundaries that would have prevented your pressure cooker from going off.

Not that these boundaries would have prevented all the pain, mind you. It *is* gonna be painful to say no, but the thing you gotta keep in mind is that the pain of saying no in the moment is *far* less than the pain when that no comes out later. I can't say it'll never happen, but I bet you wouldn't be throwing nobody's clothes out the damn window if you just stood your ground, knew your worth, healthily put up your boundaries, and told them *no* in the first place.

When I was younger, I had no idea what having boundaries meant. I didn't even think about it growing up, not until I was in my twenties. Boundaries come *after* you decide a few things. What is the life that you want to live? How do you want to *feel* every day? How do you want to *experience* life? That all stems from your perception of self-worth—what do *you* deserve? What do *you* want? *Then* you create boundaries so that you can keep things out that *infringe* upon how you want to live your life. Boundaries are there to *protect* the sacred space of how you want to live your life. And thinking of them from that perspective helps us use boundaries as a way of protecting what's most sacred to us. *That* is the true power of setting boundaries, and without a strong and healthy self-esteem, they won't ever stand.

Just look at the kings and queens of Hollywood. Love them or hate them, there's no denying those are people that have *mastered* not being people pleasers. And you know why? Because they have recognized their own worth and realized that their self-worth does not affect how people feel about them. We *love* to talk about those in Hollywood like they're our best friends. We love to say, "Oh, so-and-so, she was such a *bitch*. Oh, he was such an *asshole*." Probably because they didn't stop to autograph your picture or shake your hand, right? But you know that ain't right. I had a moment like that just last weekend. I was in Dallas, and as I was walking into a store, these two women came up to me.

"Oh, hi! How are you?"

I said, "Hi, nice to meet you."

"Can we have a picture?"

"Yeah, of course."

"Of course?" She turns to her friend and she goes, "See, I've met other famous people, but they're just assholes. They always say no like they're in a rush or something."

I didn't say this out loud, but what I was *thinking* was *Lady, you got this all wrong. They're not assholes. They're in a rush. They simply cannot please you in this moment.* A lot of powerful, successful people get this reputation of being assholes or bitches because of situations exactly like this. So ask yourself this: Would they be this successful if they *didn't* have the boundaries that they have? Stop thinking of them as assholes who didn't give you a signed picture that day, but as people who have learned to *master* having appropriate boundaries.

The same goes for me as I'm interacting with my own beloved viewers and followers. What I see on a daily basis is that I'm both the best person on earth and the worst person on earth. People say horrible things about me regularly. And they say nice things about me regularly. So if I attached my self-worth to what people thought about me, and tried to make sure people always liked me, my self-worth would go up and down. It used to be that I'd have days where I'd do an amazing video that thousands watched. There'd be twenty thousand comments, smiles, and hearts showered down on me. And then that one raggedy bitch who probably ain't got a sofa or a man to sit on it with would have some shit to say about me, and that would ruin my damn day. Why? Because I attached my sense of self-worth to the idea that everyone approved of me—another form of people pleasing. And when you associate your worth with who likes you and who accepts you today, that's a really flimsy place to be. It fluctuates, and all it's gonna do is drive you headfirst into the ground.

Without these strong and healthy boundaries, there's a tendency for us passive-aggressive people to think from a very "woe is me" mentality. *I do everything for everyone, and no one cares about me.* That shit. Have you ever given that speech? Do you have a history of doing things you don't want to do? Do you have a history of feeling like you do *more* for other people than they do for you? Have you ever asked someone to make you a martyr for all the unrecognized stuff you do? I have. And what I always tell people is to ask themselves those questions in the context of the last thirty days. How much time and energy did you spend doing things that you *didn't* want to do, all because you said yes to someone when you needed to say no?

Write down all of these instances, small or big and everything in between. How did it feel when you did each of those things that you didn't want to do? Write that down, too. Then take a nice, hard look. You see, for me, journaling in this way—writing down specific questions to myself and then answering them—was helpful because I could see the issue on the page as I was writing. I saw, *oh shoot. There's that self-esteem thing, that people-pleasing thing popping up again.* It became real to me through putting pen to paper. It allowed me to be open with myself when those feelings came up rather than just reacting to them in the moment. It allowed me to get comfortable talking to *myself* about this issue so that I could take the next step toward opening up to someone else about my issue. Journaling allows you to look your issue in the face, in your own handwriting, to see that it still all comes down to you.

Why are *you* saying *yes*? If you're doing so much more for everyone else than they are for you, then why the *fuck* haven't you stopped yet?

Well—easy to say, less easy to do. But we have to. We have to learn to say *no*.

Right now, we need to get comfortable with what I call the "no as a complete sentence" culture. No *is* a complete sentence. No *is* a final word. But you gotta deal with the parts of your self-worth that make you uncomfortable saying no in the first place, or that no ain't gonna hold up too long.

"No as a complete sentence" means that when you say no, it doesn't need an explanation. Too often we say no and then we feel like we gotta explain *why* we said no—like we have to give a reason for us putting up healthy boundaries. Uh-uh, none of that—and here's why: That's that people-pleasing shit rearing its ugly head again. And remember, that stems from a lack of feeling confident in our self-worth. It stems from not feeling comfortable putting up healthy boundaries. If you tell somebody no but feel like you've got to give an explanation after, then what you're really doing is indirectly communicating to them that you believe you need to *justify* your no to them. Like saying no by itself ain't enough. What's more is when people know that you believe you have to justify your no to them, that means they have the power to convert that no to a yes. And they *will* try. Doesn't matter who they are or whether their intentions are positive or negative. That shit is irrelevant. It could be your kids. It could be your coworkers. It could be your *spouse*. It could be the car salesman trying to sell you a lemon—anybody. It could even be *well-meaning* people who love you. And those who don't, well, they *especially* will see that as an open door. But the *problem* is that people don't wanna just say no, because you can't say no and still be concerned with people pleasing. Because by default, you will *have* to disappoint some people in order to stop people pleasing. You don't have to *like* saying no, but you have to be okay with the *idea* of no. You have to be okay with standing your ground and saying no more often, bit by bit if you don't feel ready to go cold turkey. Toss out that old-ass milk. You can't drink that shit no more.

A tip to ease into this process is to choose your form of no carefully. Choose a way of saying it that works for you, based on where you are within your growth. Maybe the no is a text message. Maybe it's a quick call. Maybe it's a face-to-face encounter. If you're stressing, sitting here and thinking, *Oh Lord, it's so hard for me to say no to my sister, or my cousin, or my whoever to their face,* well, why do you have to say it to their face? They got a phone? Do they text? Bingo. Just get it out.

Don't judge *how* you do it, just make sure you do it, and make sure that it doesn't require too much more than just no. A little pizzazz is fine, but as a rule for myself, if I go over five words in that sentence, I've said too much. Remember: Boundaries don't need to be explained. You know they're there for a reason, and that should be good enough for anyone who comes into your life.

It may not feel good when others don't approve of you, but it's still not a requirement that they do so. In fact, detaching from them *frees* you in another way. It frees you to choose for yourself. What are the things that build my own self-worth? What do *I* like about me? I want you to take this lesson to heart: It's all interconnected. Self-worth, lack of boundaries, and people pleasing—they're all in the same damn circle, supplying and feeding off each other with all their pressure, shame, and guilt.

We're gonna end that cycle.

Take Action to Get the F*ck Out Your Own Way

Ask yourself, *What is my earliest memory of being a people pleaser? What purpose and reason did it serve then?*

Forgive yourself for that. Then, like whatever's in the very back of your refrigerator, throw that shit out.

Then ask yourself, *How much time and energy did I spend doing things that I didn't want to do, all because I said yes to someone when I needed to say no?*

Write down all of these instances, big or small. Then ask yourself, *How did it feel when I did each of those things that I didn't want to do? Write that down, too. Then take a nice, hard look.*

As a last step, practice saying NO—in as few words as possible. What's the best way to say no for you?

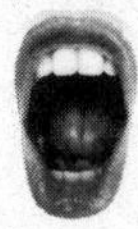

4

You Gotta Give Others Your Guidebook

Once you decide that a change needs to happen, that something within *you* needs to change, now we can talk about how, and that is by *giving others your guidebook.* Not a literal book, but a road map telling people how to treat you, because listen up: There ain't no person on earth who is inherently aware of your needs. Not your mama, not your papa, not your partner, siblings, no one. Whether it's from past trauma or self-esteem issues, so many people have a hard time saying exactly what they need—what they require. Yes, I'm talking to you. You have *requirements,* and no, you can't exchange that for another, sweeter-sounding word because that's you pandering to others. Tell them what you need, and they can take it or leave it.

Your guidebook sets down your boundaries and tells people who you are; it shows them how to treat you and it *empowers* them to win at cultivating this relationship or friendship between the two of you. Giving others your guidebook means that you are not expecting people to treat you any different than how you tell them—which I know for a fact people do because of how many people write to me about this. Expecting people to treat you differently than how *you* tell them to is asinine. It is *stupid*.

Now, this isn't to say there isn't a basic standard of human decency we should afford to others—because there is. We should treat others how we want to be treated as a rule, but this goes beyond that. This is specific to *you* and how you function and process things. This is you saying, *This is how I expect to be treated by you.* Ain't no one gonna know any of those specifics inherently.

Let's face it: Most of the time what we're doing is treating people in a way that is a projection of our own insecurities, fears, or feelings; or how we're treating people is a reflection of how we perceive that others view us. And let me tell you something: I was *notorious* for doing this shit. I was notorious for thinking, *I'm not gonna tell you how to treat me. I'm gonna wait for you to figure it out yourself, and if you don't, I'm gonna passive-aggressively let you know what you did wrong.* That meant not calling people back for days or weeks at a time—that silent treatment shit—or saying, "No worries, I see how they wanna be," when, really, I'm *all* worried. That is *the* most toxic bomb ever created. I did all of that shit. I *used* it as a fucking power move because at my deepest level, me not saying anything about how to treat me was because I *anticipated*, through my trauma, that this would not work. I *anticipated* that they were gonna hurt me anyway, so I self-sabotaged preemptively to give myself a reason to end things when they inevitably did fuck up. I gave myself an excuse to let go of them before they could let me go, and what I realized, unconsciously, was that I was setting them up to fail rather than empowering them to win—aka I wasn't giving them my guidebook. I was doing just the opposite. I shut my guidebook in their face. So who did I have to blame for the end of those relationships, for those fractures in my friendships? *Me.* Because while they may have fucked up, done some bad shit, or whatever, *I* was the one who paved the path for them to hurt me in the way I'd predetermined they would.

One of the *biggest* reasons I hear from people about why they don't want to tell others their boundaries is that they have a fear of being rejected. I get it. I *was* that person, the person who felt literal *pain* from my own fear. That trepidation, it can cause you to shake. It can upset your stomach. It can be like looking at a hot stove and knowing you can't touch that without experiencing a fucking bucketload of pain. It is *paralyzing*, but you know what? It ain't no way to live your life. If you're stuck in your fear, you ain't living. You are *existing*, but you ain't living. You are stuck in a cycle of fear, anger, hurt, and abuse—and the worst thing is, you are doing it to yourself.

Let me say that again.

You are doing it to yourself.

If you've ever wondered why you're in a relationship where the only constant is you being treated like less than, you've done it to yourself. If you've ever told yourself how lucky you are to have someone that wants to spend time with you, or that you're lucky you're not alone, you've done it to yourself. You've put yourself in this emotionally damaging cycle because you are *afraid* of showing up as who you are. You are *teaching* others that they can treat you the same way—by making you afraid, making you fear losing them.

As a person who struggled with self-esteem and all things of that nature, I was living in this cycle throughout my twenties, and what kept me from speaking my truth was the feeling of needing *validation*. I needed to feel like someone *wanted* me. I craved it.

You ever seen that movie *Coming to America* and the scene with that woman standing on one leg going, "Whatever you like"? I always wanted to be so *polite*, so *nice*, so *whatever you like* all the fucking time.

When I started dating, I was the *sweetest* person on earth. I wanted to be wanted. I wanted to be *desired*, and I thought that the best way to achieve that would be through going with the path of least resistance, by not setting boundaries. I interpreted communicating my boundaries as an opportunity for resistance and rejection, as a chance for them to say, "Uh-uh, I'm good. I don't want you if I gotta do all that." Like my relationship was a fucking salary negotiation. A lot of people don't ask for more money because they think the job offer's gonna be taken away. And I was the same way in relationships. I didn't communicate my boundaries because I thought my partners would leave me. I thought they would *reject* me if they knew what I really needed.

The idea of being rejected was something I went above and beyond to avoid. I didn't tell them what I needed because *not* telling them allowed me to both have them *and* indirectly be in control. Because if they didn't know what I needed, then they couldn't reject me. And that gives me the upper hand—right?

NO.

In fact, this behavior set the stage for me to go through some really bad experiences with some really good people. Even good people can and *will* hurt you simply because they don't know your boundaries. They may not *know* that they're hurting you because you haven't given them your guidebook. It's both funny and tragic that the one thing you purposefully kept from them in order to keep them by your side is what makes you lose them in the end.

What it comes down to is choosing your pain. I ain't gonna sugarcoat this for y'all: You have to pick your poison. One way or another, it's gonna hurt. Whether it's the pain of not getting what you need and endlessly getting hurt in relationships that are dependent on your fear *or* the pain of being rejected *because* you put up your boundaries and stuck with them is up to you. Personally, the pain of my own needs getting ignored was much worse than the pain I felt from rejection, so I chose to stick to my boundaries to get my needs met. I chose to tell people what I needed and leave it up to them to take it or leave it. But that choice and that behavior didn't come overnight.

We look inside ourselves for our answers. That's where our truth lies. So when you decide to make your boundaries, your first step is always gonna be to come back to yourself and deal with the fears in your mind. There are a couple things to take stock of. First of all, ask yourself, *What is the outcome that I fear having most?*

That's the first thing you need to identify, whether you're gonna write it down or say it out loud to yourself. What is the scariest outcome here? *I fear that if I tell this guy I'm just starting to date that he can't continue being an hour and a half late to dinners and blame work, or whatever the fuck he's blaming it on, then he's going to reject me.* Just identify it. Just call it. Say, *That's my fear.*

Then, the next thing to ask yourself is "How likely is this to happen, and what evidence do I have that would support that this is the likely outcome?" *It's a possibility in my mind, but what evidence do I have? Has he told me that if I ever call him on being late to dinner that he's not gonna fuck with me anymore?* It sounds very sterile and cognitive, but it's helpful to think in this way because it demystifies the fear and helps you identify your anxiety. Anxiety is the fear of what has not yet happened.

Not letting anxiety paralyze you is the goal here. And to do that, go backward again and say, *Where in my past was I hurt when I communicated my needs? Where was I hurt?*

My anxiety stemmed from moments in my childhood when my family would argue and there would be deafening tension in the house. Being able to *identify* those moments and then pull yourself out and think, *What evidence do I have to support that the person in my life now is going to do the same thing?* is the key here. That's how to identify your worst fear, and where it's rooted in real experiences. But just because you have a fear that's rooted in real experiences from your past, that don't mean it's gonna come true again. And if you look at the patterns of whoever you're thinking of—really, really look close at them without bias—and see that there isn't any evidence that says they would react negatively to you putting down your boundaries and asking for what you need, then you can just let go of that anxiety.

And don't think you gotta do this all alone. For some people, sitting alone with their thoughts is *terrifying*. Write it down. Or talk about this with a trusted friend or family member. Look into therapy or personal coaching. Writing or talking out your deep fears takes the sting off it now that you're simply able to communicate it in some way. It's more of an exercise for you to be able to say it out loud and get some feedback at the same time. Get your Amen Crew, your Accountability Corner, or those one or two people you deeply trust, and get those intimate matters out of your head.

Remember that communicating one's needs is *not* the same as creating opportunities for rejection. Yes, the chance of rejection is there, but it was always there. We thought we could shrink it underneath our silence, but we were just fooling ourselves. Rejection is *always* present, no matter how you twist and fold yourself to fit into a neat little box. And look at it this way:

They want you. That's why they offered you something in the first place. So it doesn't hurt to say what *you* want. More importantly, if laying down your boundaries does make them run away, then they did you a favor! Why would you want a person in your life who *won't* respect you, your boundaries, and what *you need*? It's not about keeping as many people in our lives as we can no matter what—it's about keeping *the right* people in our lives.

Let me share another tip with y'all real quick, since we're on the topic of fearing rejection. We fear that setting boundaries will make us less desirable, but in my life, I've seen just the opposite. Communicating my boundaries has actually worked out to make me *more* desirable. You know why? Because anytime people have *all* access to you, anytime anyone can do anything they want to you knowing it ain't gonna make you budge, it *lowers* your value to them. But when people know *this is my boundary*, that *they can't treat me this way*, and *this is how I need to be treated because this is very important to me*, it *raises* your desirability in their eyes. It lets them know that you value yourself—because why should anyone else value you if you don't put value in yourself? Why should someone else treat you better than you treat yourself? And how will they know that you're serious about how you want to be treated unless you model that behavior for them first? Boundaries let people know that they can't fuck you around, that there are lines drawn here and there are consequences to crossing them. And, for you, once you establish those boundaries and draw those lines, *if* they get crossed, it'll hurt, but it'll hurt a lot fucking less than if you'd never set those boundaries at all.

What's worse: Being rejected by someone who is aware of your boundaries and *chooses* not to honor them, or being hurt by a good person who is simply not *aware* of your boundaries? As someone who has been on the receiving end of both, I know my answer. I would rather give a good person the opportunity to treat me the way I need to be treated and set the stage up front around that.

That's when you can begin cultivating your guidebook.

First of all, **you gotta know what you want to put in your guidebook**. How do I know when one of my boundaries is being crossed? The greatest barometer for measuring that is your feelings. Take inventory of your feelings. Pay attention to them. When someone says something or does something, pay attention to how you feel. Am I uncomfortable? Am I unhappy? Your own feelings will be the *first* to notify you when your boundaries are crossed, and there won't be no questioning of it, either. You will *know* because feelings don't lie.

Second, **when someone crosses a line, don't react immediately**. Contrary to popular belief, you don't have to *do* anything about the violation immediately—and believe me, that is something I still have to work on and will for the rest of my life. While your feelings are still fresh, that is not the time to talk. Because if you do, you'll be speaking not from your feelings about the violation, but from the feelings about whatever trauma or unresolved wound you have that caused that boundary to be there in the first place. You're speaking from a place of *hurt*, and that will cause you to lash out in a way that ain't gonna solve anything.

Say you're standing in line at a car rental, and you picked out a nice BMW days ago. You scheduled it all online, now you're just there to pick it up. But when you get up there, the person at the counter goes, "I just wanted to let you know, we don't have a BMW, but we have a Nissan Sentra. I forgot to notify you. I'm sorry."

But now you're angry. And you might cuss them out, set them straight, and experience what I call an "emotional high" out of that experience. It's *thrilling* to call someone out and put them in their place. But really, what you're mad at is that you feel violated the same way that you felt violated as a child when your needs weren't being met by a parent or a caregiver or someone else. It's an important distinction to recognize, and it's a skill we have to hone, being able to take the time to separate your feelings about the hurt and emotional wounds you've experienced in the past that are being reengaged in this instance from your actual feelings about the incident itself.

That high you might get means nothing when it destroys your relationships and friendships. Maybe not so much with the clerk at the car rental, but if you continue that behavior pattern, the adrenaline will ultimately end up ruining the connections you have with your friends, family, and business partners. Those people who love you are petrified. So they start walking on eggshells, they start monitoring every little thing they do so as to not piss you off, and those relationships become less authentic.

Down the line, the consequences only grow. You start having trouble developing new relationships. It gets hard to meet people. It gets hard to keep them around because any little fuck-up, you're blaming them. And it doesn't end, not until you learn to work on your approaches and change them. Not until you start communicating your boundaries and stop holding people accountable for crossing lines they didn't even know existed.

Third, you need to know how to **communicate your boundaries with empathy**. This is the most important thing I've *ever* learned about boundaries. It's about overcommunicating on the front end with empathy, understanding, and compassion. Focus your words on *you*. Use lots of "I" statements to take the load off the other person, so they don't feel like you're attacking them. Communicate in a way that tells the other person that *you* understand where they're coming from and you want *them* to understand where you're coming from.

Your boundaries are acceptable. There's nothing wrong with them. We guarantee ourselves that *none* of our boundaries will be met if we don't *communicate* them. Sure, *everyone* can't meet them—but *no one* will meet them if you we don't communicate them. And everyone isn't meant to meet them; not everyone is meant to be in our lives, and our boundaries help us figure out who those people are who don't belong. So take a step back and let go of always being so emotionally charged. Teach others how to treat you in a compassionate way, and trust me, the benefit will be far more for you than for anyone else.

***

Once you've decided that having healthy, whole relationships in your life is a priority, and that to have that you must communicate your boundaries, then you need to understand that you play a big part in that. I didn't know how to communicate my boundaries to others in an empathetic, compassionate way. It was *foreign* knowledge to me. I grew up learning to navigate the world through anger, through rudeness. I learned to use my anger to my advantage, to put people in their place, to get them to listen to me, to get what I wanted—in relationships, in business, you name it. That was how I grew up. That was how I began to see the world and the people in it. I still have to unlearn that shit every day. I probably will until the day I die.

Because I grew up using anger as my tool for communication, I can tell you learning to share my guidebook in an empathetic way was *not* easy. I've fucked up a lot of people for the wrong reasons. They crossed a boundary—one they didn't know existed because I didn't tell them—and something would light up inside of me and I'd just go *at* them. I'd rip them to shreds. And I felt great, for a minute. Then—and if you've ever done something like this, you know what I mean—I'd look at them. They'd look horrible, shocked and confused. But the thing that hit me, the thing that shocked *me* into understanding what I was doing, was the *surprise* my outburst elicited from them after I fucked them over. It was always the same. This look, this expression of complete astonishment and confusion and bewilderment, like, *What the fuck just happened? Where did that come from?*

I would feel awful seeing them look like that, and what drove me crazy was that I didn't know why. I had to go to therapy to learn that the reason I felt so bad once the adrenaline wore down was because I never told them what was coming. I had a complete movie produced in my head starring me and them. In my head, I was telling myself that they were crossing a line and that if they kept on, they were gonna *get it.* But here's the thing. It never *left* my head. It never actually got to the person it was meant to reach. Now they feel like they were just blindsided by my reaction, no warning, nothing. They look horrible. They feel horrible. *I* feel horrible, and deservedly so. Because there ain't nothing fair about fucking someone up for doing something they didn't know was crossing your untold boundary.

Once you realize this, the key is being able to ask yourself, *Have the benefits of the way that I have been dealing with my life, in terms of how I deal with people, outweighed the obvious downsides?* And be really honest with yourself about the downsides. Think about the relationships that are hurt. Think about how your kids interact with you during tough times. Does it feel inauthentic or distant? Think about the fear they have toward you. Think about how coworkers navigate you. Think about all those things. And ask yourself: *Are the benefits that I'm getting from being this rattlesnake, this perpetually angry person—are the benefits outweighing it?*

Then you have to ask, *Is this worth it? Is this benefiting my life and my relationships?* No matter how wrong I think everybody else is, how isolating is this life gonna be if I'm the only right person? If everybody else is always wrong, then is being the person always right worth being alone?

For me, it wasn't that I dealt with it by silencing my voice. I dealt with this by more proactively communicating my needs so that I didn't have to get to the point of being the angry person. Because angry people like this are not people who wake up and get out of bed that way. We are simply people who did not learn that it's okay to proactively communicate our needs. And therefore, by the time our needs do come out, we're already, like, at a fucking thousand.

In my thirty-eight years, I've learned a few things, and one of them that I know to be true is that most people have the same desire for peace within their lives that you and I do. There are very few people out there *looking* to cross boundaries and intentionally rile someone up; the rest step on these boundaries because ain't no one out here communicating their needs! Now, look, I bet you have a story in your head, either about yourself or about someone you know, where another person *did* try to fuck with you intentionally, did fuck with your peace just because they wanted to, blah blah blah. I ain't saying *no one* is doing that. But the majority of folks aren't. That's what you gotta understand.

Most of the time, you and the person you're butting heads with want the same thing. Peace in your life, peace in their life. We have to be compassionate to people about understanding that, in most cases, people's desire is not to hurt, inconvenience, or be nasty to you. It's more than likely they just haven't learned the tool kit. So have compassion for them and for yourself. That doesn't mean letting them off the hook, but be empathetic. Have compassion. Understand where they're coming from. We're all looking to maintain our own Sacred Place of Peace.

I had a situation with a business colleague where we would have the most *fabulous* productive conversations in person or on the phone. But the minute we got to texting, boom, we'd start arguing. He'd ask me, "Why can't you be more polite?" to which I'd counter, "Well, why can't you be not a fucking asshole?" I couldn't figure out why the hell we were always arguing on these damn texts.

Finally, after one knockdown drag-out, he was pissed. I was pissed. And I finally thought, *What is the common thing here?*

The common thing is you never told him how to treat you. You never told him what your needs are from the beginning. Then the next logical question to ask myself was *Well, how can I correct that?* Stepping back from the situation like that, taking inventory of what my needs were that weren't being met, allowed me in this moment to correct my stance.

Bam, a *lightbulb* went on. That thought empowered me to say to him, "I don't think that I'm able to fully interpret the emotional nuances of your text messages when we're talking about important issues." I got *real* HR with it. Then I said, "I'm going to make a request, and that request is not for you to change or for me to change—but what I *will* ask, however, is can we change how we approach each other? I've noticed a thing. We tend to get into disagreements in text. Can we please just hold off until we can talk on the phone or in person rather than trying to have important conversations through text?"

And we were able to have that exchange. That's the key, teaching people how to treat you—and giving them the guidebook on how to treat you is really just empowering them to be able to treat you the way that you desire to be treated *and* to tell you what they desire in return. In that way, both of you work with each other to meet in the middle, and no one has to feel bad about the way that they are.

Now, you gotta remember that these moments where you give someone else a look at your guidebook are *different from* "I'm asking you this so you can stop fucking annoying me." Don't make it about them. This guidebook is about *you*. Giving it to others means *you're* taking responsibility. It means you're saying, "I'm asking you this because this is who I am, and this is *where* I am." Your request should not be a backhanded critique of them, which, I get, is very easy to do. Just remember that a big part of this is being able to take *full* ownership of why this is important to you.

The other person should not be criticized or picked apart or minimized or belittled in any way because they have nothing to feel bad about for not knowing it in the first place *if* you did not tell them. People know what they know, and they don't know what they don't know. But if you want to put your relationships in a place to win, you need to choose to disclose. You need to disclose what your needs are, no matter how uncomfortable it is. You need to share your guidebook and share it in a way that's honest and criticism-free and that empowers others to communicate their own to you.

Giving your guidebook does not equate to looking down on others for not being able to read your mind, because ain't no one who can do that. Sometimes, how you let them treat you is defined by how you react. Remember, people are really only familiar with what *their* needs are. They need to test the waters to figure out yours, and it doesn't make them selfish. It doesn't make them bad. It doesn't make them self-centered. It's just that we all see the world through our own eyes and through our own experiences.

Most people are not crossing your boundaries out of a malicious place. They're doing it out of the fact that they ain't got no guardrails, so they're just walking straight for the boundary line blind as a bat. But instead of dishing out those consequences, step back and ask yourself, *What information could I have shared with this person to avoid this moment? If I could turn back the clock an hour, a day, what could I have given them to have empowered them to not do this?* Give them the chance to step *back* behind the line and stay there if they wish. There's no guarantee that they're going to apply it or do it even if you tell them, but there's a hell of a much bigger chance this way than if you *never* tell them. That chance will always be zero. This way, you've got a fifty-fifty shot.

Most people don't want to be confrontational. They don't *want* to have to get all up in someone's face because a boundary was crossed, but we do it because our peace has been fucked with. But remember—everyone else wants peace, too. They have that same desire, and if you and I are about to strangle them and cuss them out, we ain't doing anyone any favors. We are hurting them, and we are hurting ourselves. Instead, let's empower them to get what they want so that we can also get what we want.

Take Action to Get the F*ck Out Your Own Way

Ask yourself, *What are my boundaries?* Take a deep look at the way you've been dealing with your life, with the people in your life, your reactions, your anger that may sit just underneath the surface waiting to burst. And ask yourself, *Have the benefits of how I approach life and people outweighed the downsides?*

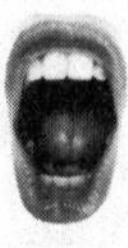

5

Don't Chase People—Know When to End It

Our lack of boundaries presents another issue: chasing others. Once we begin to put up our boundaries and tell others what we want, what we *need*, we can also begin to show up for ourselves in terms of our relationships. When we know our boundaries and know how to tell others how to treat us, we will learn how to protect our Sacred Place of Peace, which we talked about earlier, which will greatly improve both our own stress levels and our relationships with other people. It's hard to do one without the other. In fact, it's *impossible*. These concepts connect, like how your calf, knee, and thigh muscles are interconnected. Tear one and the whole leg falls apart. One can't function without the other. It's the same with telling others who you are and knowing when not to chase.

Knowing when not to chase people comes from accepting yourself and liking what you see. And for that matter, it comes from accepting parts of yourself that you *don't* like as well, without apologizing for them. Accepting who you are unequivocally is the culmination of what we've been talking about: After you understand what your boundaries are, after teaching others how to treat you, after becoming more comfortable with yourself, after telling others, "This is what I can and can't do"—only *then* do you really feel at home in your own skin.

Think about seasoned citizens for one second. I bet there's someone in your life—who is probably of a certain age—that you joke about, saying, "Well, Shirley Mary said she don't like your outfit. She just says anything." We talk about these seasoned citizens like this because it's *true.* They don't hold back because they're so comfortable with their thoughts and their opinions. And that *allows* them to say what's on their mind in a way that is honest and clear. So when Shirley Mary says she don't like your outfit, she's being literal. She don't think that's the best look for you. You just need to believe her. And *that* level of confidence and comfort in ourselves is something that we should all aspire to at a much earlier age. We should work to achieve that, which comes once we've done the work within ourselves to feel comfortable saying, "No, this is who I am." And when you are comfortable with who you are, you're able to say that in a way that doesn't come across as abrasive to other people.

Let me tell you something: Before I was comfortable with

who I was, I was an *infamous* chaser. Chasing friends, chasing lovers, or whoever I thought might leave me. There are so many ways of chasing. I wasn't the raggedy girl who would call and text "good morning" eleven times, or the one that would come fetch your ass to death. But I *was* the "I'm gonna chase you with this *good cochina*." That meant I'm going to throw it on you *so good* that you can't resist me. I'm going to do all these things to *show* you that I *show up* in a relationship. I cooked. I cleaned. I fucked like a goddess.

It ain't bad to show up in a relationship. But the moment you *overextend* showing up to the point of creating an unrealistic representative of yourself—also called a front or façade—then *that's* when it becomes detrimental to you and your relationships. For me, my representative looked like showing up as my hyper-nurturing essence of femininity. Like I was the goddamn Mother *Earth*, honey! I did all this stuff, and I was so, *so* non-confrontational. I was always saying shit like "No, I understand" to *project* the image that I was incredibly tolerant when inside of me was a raging bull just waiting to get out. And that shit is unhealthy.

If you're putting on a front or a "representative" just to attract him, her, or them, then you're only setting yourself up for rejection. Look at it like this: You're scared of getting rejected, so you create a representative—the perfect façade that you think your person will accept—to ensure the rejection does not happen. That's why you overextend yourself—out of *fear*. But the reality is that you're not actually avoiding rejection; you're setting the goddamn stage on which it will occur.

How?

Because *you're offering them something up front that's different from what you can reasonably expect to be able to maintain long term.*

Your representative may start out as a simple overextension of who you are—meaning whatever actions you would *normally* do are just on caffeine during this initial phase of dating—but they almost never stay that way. A representative is you on fucking steroids twenty-four seven. It is unsustainable. It can easily *morph* into a version of you that is inauthentically you; it becomes a powerful projection that you constantly have to work at to maintain. And when you can't maintain that representative long term, *that's* when you'll start to hear the oh-so-common grievance: "You've changed. I fell in love with you for this, but now you're not doing that anymore."

Sound familiar?

That's how this shit typically happens—one person wasn't being their true self in the beginning of the relationship, and they weren't able to maintain that façade long term. Your representative, which you so carefully cultivated to ensure this did not happen, *made* this happen. You created a picture-perfect silver stage upheld by weak legs, and now you're surprised it came crashing down. And it may look a little something like this:

Let's just call a thing a thing. When a relationship moves out of the honeymoon phase and reality sets in, people become more of *who they already were.* It's really easy to be hot and heavy in the beginning of a relationship where you're both like, "Oh, I love you and I love having two hours of pillow talk after we have sex." But you may find after the honeymoon period is over that the *reality* is that's not really who they are. After sex they may just want to go to sleep or have only ten minutes of cuddles. But at the start it's all "I love talking everything through with you. I'm such a great communicator, blah blah blah." Fast-forward a year or two later and it's like, "We never talk about anything." Honey, it's because they're finally showing you *who* they are and not just who their representative is. But that shit eventually crumbles. Now, the *more* emotionally mature and available someone is, the less of a gap there will be between their representative and the reality of who they are.

When you've built the foundation of your relationship out of your fear of rejection and sustained it with these behaviors, you literally have to *force* yourself to play this role of the make-believe version of yourself day in and day out. That shit is *not* sustainable. You started out with this representative, and you didn't know how to stop doing it. Now your relationship has suffered. That comes from the fact that we often can't even *see* that we're chasing.

Remember, chasing comes in many forms. When we overfunction by way of our representatives. When we make ourselves too available, moving our schedules around to accommodate folks who don't accommodate us in return. When we push past our boundaries just to make the other person feel wanted and invited into our lives. When we lower our standards and lower our needs or don't communicate our needs. Those are *all* examples of chasing, and each of us has our own version.

So, don't sit around thinking, *I ain't like Debbie because Debbie calls so-and-so fifty times a day! I don't do that. I ain't like that, so I don't chase.* No, honey, you might still be a damn chaser. You may just have a different style of chasing, so listen up and see if these patterns fit what you do.

But don't worry. I'm about to show you how you can shut down those representatives and show up—truly and authentically—for yourself and your future relationships. The first thing we have to ask ourselves is *Why do I chase?* Maybe your way of chasing is over-functioning or being too readily accessible. So the fear is *if I'm not available to them, then they might leave. If I don't over-function and show up and prove to them that I'm the best thing ever, then they are not going to stay. I'm going to be abandoned.* I'll tell y'all right here and now: What we often think of as fear of rejection is almost always fear of *abandonment.* You don't want this person to not want you. It's a fear of *not being wanted.* And it was *exactly* what I was doing in my relationships throughout my twenties.

Chasing someone also teaches you to vilify that person. It creates thoughts in your mind that they don't want you even though you're breaking your back to get them, which *will* make you resent them along the way. You will see them as the villain of your story when the truth of the matter is, the real villain is *you.* You're victimizing yourself within this process, *but* you're also victimizing the other person because you're showing a level of effort and attention that is not sustainable—giving them hope for something that can never really be. If you ultimately get what you want from them—which is their time, their attention, and their affection—then you're not going to be able to sustain it.

Now that you've asked yourself why you chase and you recognize it, that's a great first step. *I desire to be desired. I desire to be wanted. I desire to not be rejected.* Whatever your root is, identifying it takes the power out of the chase because it helps you realize when you fall into this pattern of behavior. Eventually, you will be able to recognize a situation in which the temptation to chase is staring you in the eyes, so you can say, "Whoa, hang on." You can stop yourself because you realize this action that you're about to take out of habit is not really about the other person, and you can ask yourself, *When I did this in the past, has it ever turned out positively? Did it achieve the outcome that I desire?*

One of the greatest ways to correct and change our behavior is to look at past situations. If the answer is yes, then by all means, keep doing it. But if the answer is *no*, then don't fucking do it. Because that behavior ain't *you.* That's your representative talking, and we're about to cut its fucking life supply off right now, honey, because it is time for *you,* your natural form, your full authentic self, to take shape and find life.

You're gorgeous, sweetie.

You're *handsome,* honey.

You're all of these wonderful things, but here's the thing—and it's gonna step on some of y'all's toes, but here it is: You're not getting what you want out of these relationships because you come across as desperate. And don't nobody want to do nothing with somebody who's desperate! You're communicating to everyone out there that *you* don't know your own *value*, so why the fuck would you expect anyone else to see it when you can't yourself? The only way to communicate your value is to set clear boundaries around where you're going to place your effort.

People can *sense* desperation. But on the other hand, they can also sense *authenticity*. And you know what else? Seeing someone be authentic and sincere has its own power. It actually makes them like you a little bit *more*. They'll think, *I'll ride with this because you're just being honest.* There is something *attractive* about that shit.

I'll tell you a story. When I was going through this realization and trying to accept who *I* was, I had a revelation. See here, back in the day, I had a way of doing things. I would meet a man, go out once or twice, and eventually I'd say to him, "Come over to the house, and I'll cook for you." Now, I can cook my *behind* off, baby. So my method for dating was *cook 'em good, fuck 'em good, and then hook 'em good.* He wouldn't go *nowhere*, because it didn't matter what size my home was, it's always been designed to suck a man in. But I'd been learning over time that I kept ending up in these fucked-up-ass situationships and relationships because I went too *fast.*

For me, my heart is attached to my parts down below, and in some cases that's an easy path there. I had to learn to slow down. *Do I wanna rush into this?* I had to ask myself. *Because that's never worked before! Jumping into something and you ain't even in love—you're in infatuation; you're in lust. He ain't really in love, and neither are you,* I reminded myself. *You just play the role of what he's looking for very well. 'Cause you know what these men are looking for, but do you wanna just keep playing that role for just anyone?*

When you're giving them exactly what they want, they're gonna try to lock it down quickly, which makes you feel very secure. *Ooh, he wants me, she wants me.* But I had to remind myself, *He don't even know you! So far, he just wants what you've represented in these very small moments of pleasure and comfort.*

I was in a relationship at the time of this revelation. So, one night when were together, he said, "When are you gonna cook? I'm looking forward to you cooking for me."

This was a trigger moment for *me*. A moment in which I had to ask myself if this was what I wanted, and if I would achieve what I wanted if I did what I'd always done before.

So, I said, "Oh, those bitches in the past must've dropped it that I was all about cooking, but I ain't that girl no more."

But he persisted: "So when you gonna cook for me?"

"I may never," I told him. "Not unless I feel like it. I can cook, but I don't want to cook and deal with that every day. I'm not for it."

I don't know what I was expecting, but it sure wasn't a smile.

The man *smiled* at me after I was sure he'd disapprove for not getting what he wanted. But his exact words were "I'm fucking with you."

I'm telling you, he was *all about* my authenticity. He *liked* the sincerity of me just saying, "No, that's not me. I'm not for it." Just putting it out there. That's what I did, and that's what y'all gotta start doing. Because the fact is, *that's* who's gonna show up down the road in the relationship, your real, authentic self. You can fake the funk and do all the façades in the beginning all you want, but at some point in time the real person's gonna show up. Think back to your past relationships. Hasn't that always been the case? It's impossible to uphold a façade forever. So, why even start out that way? Authenticity is key, so lead with *that* instead because then you can see who your person truly is and they can see who *you* truly are, and you can make the best decision for yourself from there about whether this is the person for you. You'll get better long-term results that way. It's so important that in relationships we show up as our authentic self and invite other people to show up as their authentic self, because it opens the door for you to see what you're actually getting after all the infatuation of newness. That approach—that "no-nonsense, this is who I am, and I accept that" approach—will be so helpful in you being your full self. What's more, when you start bringing your full self is when you'll find that it connects you to *far more* people than when you were propping up a representative you *thought* people wanted.

I used to do what I thought I needed to do to win people over.

My first time on-screen, I tried so hard to be prim and proper and move the right way, all that. But what I've learned over time is that people actually relate far more and *connect* far more when I am just who I am—that full version of myself, the me who is sometimes preppy but most times not. It's worked out in my professional life and within my private life, and it will in yours, too, if you can just let go of those representatives and be who you truly are.

For me, that means telling myself that who I am in my natural form is okay. I'm okay as I am. There's nothing wrong with me or you. You don't have to hide yourself. You don't have to disguise yourself. There is a man out there who *loves* the fact that I walk in my platform shoes with my beautiful Alexander McQueen bag and my beautiful gel-manicured fingers, and that inside of me is still a masculine man who will pop those the fuck off if it comes down to it. Let me say it again: People *sense* authenticity, and they *will* gravitate toward it. They like the essence of where your power comes from. They like who you are, so you don't need to downplay yourself.

When we chase people, we are literally robbing ourselves of a destiny where we are valued, pursued, and given the same amount and type of energy that *we* are putting forth. Do you want that? Do you *want* to be underappreciated and unseen? Of course not. So why oh *why* are you still texting them, emailing them, doing whatever you can just to get a fraction of their attention? *Stop doing that.* Your best life is waiting on you, but you can't have that life if you're chasing something that's not *designed* for you—and if it's not chasing you back and giving you the same energy that you're giving it, then it's not for you, baby! Grieve the thing, the person, and *move on*.

Do not chase men, do not chase women, do not chase clients, do not chase customers. *Do not chase.* Accept the pain of letting go of something that is not for you, that does not *serve* you, so that you can move into the *pleasure* of being able to walk within your destiny. Know that you are worth more than whatever he, she, they, them, it, is giving you. What you desire is what you deserve. And once you recognize that your value is great and powerful and inherent within you, you will *position* yourself to never chase again. Greatness—that's you, baby—does not chase.

Take Action to Get the F*ck Out Your Own Way

When it comes to chasing, knowing who you are and what you truly want is the only way to lessen the pain. What do YOU desire? Take stock of your agency and throw the ball back on their side of the court–tell them who you are, what you need, and then let them make their choice.

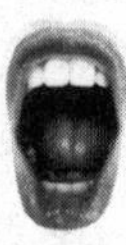

6

Rejection Is Protection

In the last chapter, we talked about how we create representatives to avoid rejection, but in many cases that very act just speeds up the process of rejection that we were running from in the first place. How many times have you heard someone say, "Oh, well, I don't do XYZ because I'm scared of getting rejected," or, "They rejected me, and that means they didn't really deserve me," or, "He, she, or they ain't worth shit because they rejected me."

These statements might have a grain of truth, but you know what else they have? Victim mentality written *all over* them. We *love* to paint ourselves as victims, especially in dating. What I've come to realize in my growth is that even if someone rejected you or broke up with you, that doesn't automatically make them a bad person. It doesn't. In fact, it is often the case that they may have identified that they don't want the same thing from you that you want from them, or that they don't see the same value in you that you see in them. So by *releasing* you, they've given you the gift of moving on to find someone who *does* see your value or who does want the same from you. It's all about *reframing* how we view rejection.

There's a similar rejection concept in the sales industry. When I first got into sales many years ago, I always had this paralyzing fear of "oh my God, I hope no one tells me no because I'm going to feel rejected." I would *hold on* to every client I had. I would cling to them like glue because I was so afraid of rejection. But over time I learned to *welcome* the nos. I *wanted* to hear the nos quickly; if the sale wasn't going well, I wanted the person on the other end of the line to just come out and say no. I didn't want no fussing around. No beating around the bush. No *wasting my time.* But the thing was, I often had to nudge them in that direction. So if I got to the point during a call that I felt like they were hemming and hawing, giving me every way but Sunday but not saying yes, I would just pause the conversation and give them my speech.

I'd say, "If you wouldn't mind, I want to make sure I'm respectful of your time and my own, and I just want to do a check-in with you. When you scheduled the call, you told me you wanted to get insurance for yourself for XYZ reasons, and I don't know if I'm misinterpreting but it seems as though that priority has changed. Maybe you don't want it. Is that the case, or should we proceed forward with an application?"

I did that because if they don't want this shit, then I'm going to get back those thirty minutes of my day so I can call somebody else and get this money. I'm here for the *outcome*. So the minute they'd say, "Well, I'm not sure," I'd take this as their way of saying no, and I'd let them go. These interactions were never malicious. It was as simple as *I need you to release me, so that I can move on to bigger and better things, so that I can stop wasting my own time*. The same goes for rejection in dating. Regardless of how you see it, it *releases* you so you can move on.

When we're able to slow down and take a look at our previous relationships that ended in rejection from this frame of mind, we see that a *lot* of these cases were people protecting us from ourselves. But the fact was that they could *see* where you were going and had the realization that where you were headed was either not where they wanted to go or not where they were capable of going. And—some of you who are still up in arms over a rejection may not like this—they had enough *respect* for themselves *and* for you to step away.

Years ago, I was with a man who worked for a package delivery service like FedEx or UPS. And one night we were canoodling, you know, still in the early stages of the relationship. Still getting to know each other. I'm lying there with him, basking in the glow, feeling real good about everything, and out of nowhere he goes: "Do you think we're really a good fit for each other?"

Talk about spoiling the *mood*! In my head I was thinking, *Who the hell has time to say this right now?* But I asked what he meant. And his tone changed.

"My goal is not to use this job delivering packages as a stepping stone. It's ain't my come-up. I'm literally here to get the retirement plan. I want to stay here as long as I can stay here. Maybe I'm capable of doing more, but to be quite honest, I'm satisfied with this. And I see where you're going. I see what you're capable of."

Honey, when he said this, I'm shaking my head, and my first instinct is to shut this shit down. I ain't want my man to worry like this. I'm thinking, *No, we're just the same.* Because through my lens we were. At the time we were making around the same money—actually, he was probably making more because he had overtime and I was on salary. So in my head, I don't see no problem. I'm thinking, *We go out. We split paying for all the dates. What's the issue?* And I told him all that; I brought up every goddamn reason why we *were* on the same page and why we fit so well together. But this man, and bless him truly, wouldn't take the bait.

He didn't disagree that we were on the same level right then, but he said, "I see where you're going in your life. And you can't see but I'm telling you. You will get tired of me eventually."

He was right. I didn't like it at the time, and boy I still tried to get him, but thank God I couldn't because he was right. He thought that he wasn't good enough for me. He would say things like "You're too good for me," "I'm so lucky to have you," "Why would you pick somebody like me?" All those phrases are warning signs. When the person you're dating says something like that, you might take it as flattery. But it's *not* flattery; it's telling you what the real deal is. It's not necessarily that he felt lucky to have me, but he was *surprised* to have me.

Ultimately, when it ended, I agreed with him. "You're right," I eventually said, because he was very threatened by the fact that I could make more money than him. I just got tired of those conversations, tired of trying to prove to him, "No, baby, you *are* good enough for me." I realized that at some point in time it *was* gonna play out, that he was gonna sabotage it to show me that I was too good for him.

When people believe that you're too good for them and you don't believe them, they will *show* you eventually, whether it's through infidelity, mistreatment, or trying to knock you down the side so that they can feel bigger or stronger than you. If someone's not secure in who *they* are, then they will try to make you insecure about who *you* are, so that at the very least they can feel more secure than you.

That's what I mean when I say rejection is protection. Sometimes people reject us because they can see the thing in them that they *know* you won't want. He was telling me, "I know what you want is not what I'm gonna give you." He could *see* early on that I was not satisfied with where I was in my career and in my lifestyle. He could see I was aiming for bigger, better, and richer.

But he also knew that trajectory was not something *he* was about, and he had enough respect for himself to walk away. He didn't want to feel insufficient when I got to where I was gonna go because he knew he was not gonna be the man I deserved or wanted. And he didn't want to put himself in that situation of being insufficient. He knew who he was, and he knew *where* he was. I *respect* that, and I also have him to thank for releasing me because I sure as shit wasn't gonna let go.

And now that we know rejection is *protection*, we're gonna talk about a certain something that's got so many of you riled up: *ghosting*. Ghosting is when someone stops talking to you abruptly, seemingly without cause, ending the relationship without ever telling you why and without ever speaking to you again. I understand that being ghosted *hurts*, and it hurts because it leaves you operating without your power. It leaves you wondering if you did something wrong or if there's something wrong with you. It is *confusing*. It is *highly immature*.

But it isn't wrong.

You heard me.

There ain't *nothing* wrong with ghosting. People have the *right* to change their mind about who they're interested in; it's the *approach* that makes y'all so bitter. The act itself is not one to be condemned because it is *not* bad; in fact, it's a valuable *skill* to know when to end things. Could the approach be better? Hell yes. But what we're missing when we focus on *their* approach is our own responsibility—too often in relationships we throw caution to the wind and let go of our own damn agency. We blind ourselves to the way people treat us, and we don't give ourselves permission to give back that *same* energy. Because like it or not, people *always* send signals, and we should all know what they are when someone's not interested in us or is on the verge of stepping away. And if you *don't* know what those signs are—let me break it down for you.

Almost no one ghosts you day one. It's always after a week or a month or a few months. It's always after a level of communication *over time* and you're just not paying attention to the signs that this could be coming. In some cases, this person is showing you signs and indicators that they are *not* where you are. And when you fail to take in the signs and indicators, often what happens is people then go with their own approach of communicating what they're so uncomfortable communicating—they ghost to avoid saying that they want to leave. *That's* when they go silent and then you're like, *Well, what the fuck just happened? They were just there and now they're not?* Well, no. They weren't there for a long time before then. They were likely slow quitting you all along, pulling away and communicating less and less, but you just ignored the signs. We just got to open our eyes and let that truth hurt because what have I been saying? The pain in that moment is nothing compared to what it *will* be if you let it build.

On the one hand, someone choosing not to tell you when they're no longer interested in you—ghosting you—is hurtful. There's no way to justify that. There's no way around that because, as people, we all want closure when our relationships of any kind end. *But* we also have to bring a level of empathy to this as well. People don't usually choose to ghost for the pure sake of hurting you. It ain't like everyone out there who has ghosted you has a personal vendetta against you. What they most likely *do* have is a lack of tools to communicate. For all you know, maybe they had a shitty childhood. Does growing up rough mean all their nasty behaviors are excused? No, sir. But it does give you *insight* into why they communicate the way they do. Say so-and-so dealt with severe consequences every time they disappointed their parent. That could *easily* morph into a debilitating fear of disappointing people, or serious issues with dealing with confrontation. You never know, but you have to be open-minded and empathetic. This doesn't mean you gotta let them off the hook for it. But you gotta be thankful. Now you've learned that he or she or they *lack* those tools to simply say, "I don't want you," and if they can't communicate effectively, then maybe it was never going to work out from the start. In that way, you know it: They're releasing you, which only protects you from pain that you'd encounter from them down the road.

When someone ghosts you, remember this: *It ain't about you.* Understand that their behavior is a reflection of where they are in their life, their communication abilities, and their maturity. It is a *gift*. It is their way of saying in zero words, *Hey, we were building toward something with real romantic intent, but I cannot continue on because I am not equipped to communicate, I am not mature enough.* And listen—it's a gift *because* they are showing you who they are early on. We've all heard the adage, "When someone tells you who they are, believe them the first time." This is an example of that. Isn't it better that you see who they are now rather than months or years down the road, wasting your time?

One of the worst things we can do after we've dodged a bullet like this is to *not* take the gift. Instead of accepting this as the gift of our valuable time back, we make excuses. "Oh no, they're busy. Oh no, this is happening. Oh no, his cat died." Baby doll, baby doll, baby doll. Life happens, but here's the thing: No one is crawling into a hole and cutting themselves off from the rest of the world. Those of us who *want* to be in relationships will find ways to communicate no matter the circumstances. And guess what? This person isn't communicating if they ghosted you or left you on read. This person is communicating with others—because we know damn well they didn't crawl in a hole and turn off all forms of communication for days or weeks at a time—but they're not communicating with *you*, so the best thing you can do is accept that and leave it.

I've been ghosted, and yes, it hurts. No, I didn't deserve it, but I have to *accept* that it happened. There is *power* in accepting that because you cannot *change* what you don't *name*. If you say you ain't been ghosted—making excuses for them for why they *haven't* reached out to you—then you won't do nothing different in your relationships the *next* time this may come up. You'll keep repeating this pattern that is only hurting *you.*

Ghosting doesn't have to be awful. But it's not exactly mature behavior, either, and we *can* take steps to lessen how frequently we get ghosted or ghost others. First, take stock of your own sense of agency. *Stop* playing the victim. *Stop* thinking, *They did this to me. I'm the victim.* I'm putting the ball back in your court. Just remember that a lot of our pain is avoidable when we're proactive about paying attention to the signs and taking our share of the responsibility to communicate.

I have found that I get *far* more happiness out of taking ownership over my own intuition. I *trust* what I feel, and I communicate what I feel. In that way, if there's something I'm missing or something comes up laced with old trauma, at least I can communicate that in a way that doesn't hold the other person accountable for it. Which means they can now be aware of my perspective, and they can tell me, "Well, this is where I'm going, and that's where I'm from. This is why I'm coming from this angle." Then I can make some alternative choices around how to move forward from there.

Preventing ghosting is all about being communicative about what it is that you're looking for and asking the other person to do the same thing. It might sound a little something like this: *You know what, I'm looking for XYZ. This is where my head is.* Then ask, *Where you at with it?* I know people say, "I don't wanna do that 'cause people can lie to you and tell you what you want to hear." Yes, they can. Yes, some might. But so what? That's not why I'm doing it. I'm doing it so that *I* can reach *you.* So that *I'm* doing *my* part.

Once you tell them, then you gotta pay close attention. I told you what *I'm* looking for, now I'm gonna pay attention to *your* response.

Are they stumbling?

Are they vague?

Are they evasive?

Pay attention, 'cause this is what's gonna protect you from being ghosted. *Recognize* the signs they're putting out there. Are you getting the same energy from them as you're giving? If their response and approach are making you question—because people will give you small signs before they go full-fledged ghost—then bring it up. Communicate that to them. Be direct, but don't detach completely. You can say something like, "Hey, you know we planned a couple dates, and I noticed for the last two days you've pushed them back or canceled them. If now is not a great time for us to get to know each other, that's fine."

Don't say *anything* about them not wanting you, even if that's where your head is. Keep that lid shut. Just say, "If now's not a great time for you, just let me know." Put that ball back in their court and let them show you the pace they want to go at. That pace might be the same as yours, and it might be different. But if there *is* a dissonance, don't put it on the back burner. Call it out—not in a vilifying type of way, but in an open and honest conversation. If you keep ignoring it, then eventually they aren't going to be there anymore, and you'll be left wondering why they left without caring to tell you, when you could have addressed it yourself to clear up any confusion or to address the warning signs that they may be pulling away.

For example, if the person you're seeing is all about texting—like they want to text every hour of every day and write whole *essays* to you and shit—and that's not your jam, well there's your dissonance. They might think they're being ghosted if they only get one-word replies back, but they're not. You're just moving at different paces. So you can say, "You know, I'm not really a great texter. I'm more of an in-person kind of person. So maybe next time we can meet." You tell them where you are, what your expectation is, and let them go from there. Don't just say, "We're not a good fit."

Own your intuition and your ability to observe what's going on so that you're not operating in a reactive mode. Be proactive. Is this person putting in energy that, to me, is remotely discernible as them wanting me? Does their energy match mine? If you're confused, ask. If the answer is not acceptable, move on. It's as simple as that, and it's *not* about vilifying the other person. Ghosting, when we really take a deeper look behind its motivations, is so much deeper than "so-and-so is a bad person." That isn't necessarily the case. They're human. They've got wants and needs and expectations, and it's okay if theirs don't match up with yours. You just got to be able to recognize if and when that is the case and know when to end it if a compromise can't be met.

No matter how much we improve ourselves, we can't always avoid people who have the potential to make us feel shitty. It's not about what you are attracting. It's about what are you *entertaining* and *keeping*. We all have the ability to attract the same level of bullshit, but the difference is the person who attracts it but doesn't entertain it, and the person who attracts it but ignores their instincts and entertains it. That's the part that is up to you, to listen to and identify this with discernment.

As humans we like to rely on our higher-order thinking, like logic, *especially* when it comes to relationships. We like to forget or ignore the fact that we're mammals and we have instincts, too—which means we often neglect our instincts. Your instincts might be screaming, "Stop doing this! Stop *doing* this!" with an added punch to the gut for good measure, and you'll keep doing it because it *feels* good. Because your logic tells you that maybe if you keep doing it, that warning feeling of *maybe I should stop* will go away—this is just you ignoring your instincts, also often known as common sense. And then you're shocked when something terrible happens even though everything was telling you to go the other way. But one of the greatest gifts I've had, which has helped my career and personal life, is to trust what I feel. You have that gut reaction for a reason, so *use* it.

Listen, rejection hurts. But we gotta remember that it doesn't mean there's anything inherently wrong with us, *or* them. So lemme just say it straight up: *Don't be a victim.* If and when y'all get rejected, don't go looking for no coddling. Don't play the victim card. Rejection is *protection.* It is a *gift.* And if you can reframe the way you think about rejection—what it does for you instead of how much it hurts—then I assure you, those positives will override the fear of being rejected.

Take Action to Get the F*ck Out Your Own Way

Run inventory on yourself. *What has actually been happening because of my choices in life and in love? Are they getting me what I want?* If the answer is no, then you need to consider what changes must be made. Seek a different approach.

As for rejection, welcome that shit! Let go of the thinking that they're doing this to spite you. Reframe your mind and find the gratefulness that they let you go to do better and bigger things. It is a gift.

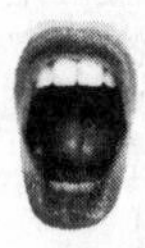

7

Dealing with the Emotionally Unavailable

We've got the tools to own our shit. We are beginning to know more about generational trauma, and we have *begun* to cultivate our guidebooks and *tell* people how to treat us. But there's *a lot* more to the world of relationships—whether they be friendships, family, romantic connections, or even connections in our business ventures—and as we dive further in, there's one *type* of person I want to shine a special light on: the emotionally unavailable.

You know the type. Maybe they're strong and silent. Maybe they're not physically or verbally affectionate. Maybe they just shut the *fuck* down when it comes to confrontation, or the only thing they can say to you when you ask them to open up is "Okay," or "I don't know." Maybe they ignore how you're feeling, how you're acting. There's no limit to how the behaviors of the emotionally unavailable manifest.

I am *sure* beyond belief that each one of you knows an emotionally unavailable person—either you dated one (or ten) or you got a family member who is, and yes, we will talk about that, or you *are* one. We'll talk about that, too. Now, some of you might feel an *immediate* wall of resistance go up just by reading those words, and if you do, just know that I am talking to *you.* If you are having a visceral reaction to this chapter, I am *talking to you.* Sit up and pay attention.

First is our romantic relationships.

Just like with ghosting, emotionally unavailable people *oftentimes* show us signs up front. In my twenties I used to think I was *so* attracted to the *laid-back* type of guys, the guys who are chill and nonconfrontational. Back then I was insecure, and I *needed* to have a sense of being in control, of being in *power.* Those types of guys *gave* that to me because they just went with whatever I wanted and never put up much of a fight, but it never worked. Ultimately, a year or so into the relationship, when it actually came time to work *through* something, all that laid-back, chill vibe and mysterious approach to things just grated on me. It was like, *can you speak the fuck up?* I've gone on for a half hour *soliloquy* to tell you about every fucking thing that *I'm* going through right now, and I've *perfectly* put this shit together. If bullet points could be verbalized words, I have *bullet-pointed* this shit out. I've *given* you the solution. And all he's got to say is, "I hear you. Okay." And I just wanted to punch him in the head, like, that's all you fucking got to say?

But then—and listen straight, y'all—I had to accept *my* part in these relationships. I had to accept that there are a couple of factors that attracted me to these people—and these things are attracting *you* to emotionally unavailable people. First, **we misinterpret the signs of emotional unavailability**. We *think* that your quietness, your laid-back nature, and your nonconfrontational attitude are a *plus*. Being nonconfrontational is *not* a plus. We think it's a plus because we mistake confrontation for rage; they're interchangeable in our minds, but they aren't in reality. They are two very different things. People need to have a *healthy* relationship with *confrontation*. Confrontation is, at the bare bones of the word, the ability and willingness to *confront* something. So we think, "Oh, this person is so nonconfrontational, which I like because they don't bring drama like my ex, like my mother, like my whoever." Listen, chile, *those* people may have had an unbalanced approach to confrontation, so maybe they were *hyper*-confrontational or *hypersensitive*. But trying to find someone who's unlike *their* drama that we're still traumatized from or annoyed by, we go out and we pick someone who's on the total *opposite* end of that—or, for that matter, the total opposite end of us if *we* are the hyper-confrontational person. By choosing someone who is *so* nonconfrontational, we think we're doing better when in reality we've just saddled ourselves with someone who does not have *any* relationship with confrontation, which means they don't know *how* to process their emotions. So we end up in these relationship situations where down the road we wonder what happened. Why aren't they the person I thought they were? What changed? *Nothing.* All that happened is our infatuation and excitement wore off, and when they are replaced by very real needs, that person ain't gonna meet them if they're emotionally unavailable.

Second, what attracts us to the emotionally unavailable is that sometimes **we are attracted to what we *believe* is our opposite because we believe that it will make the relationship *balanced*.** I used to say this myself. I'd say, *We cannot have two people like me because both of us gonna be running our mouths.* If you date someone who has a similar approach to dealing with things as you, and is *comfortable* confronting things, then those are two positives put together. If you're willing to do the work to have a healthy relationship with confronting things and being emotionally available, and you attract someone who *also* is willing to do the work for that, you can work through a number of things.

The catch?

Most people aren't ready for what they *say* they're ready for.

We're *afraid* of emotional availability, both in ourselves and in others. We are so astute at dealing with those mothers, fathers, exes, in our lives that the idea of dealing with someone who is *actually* emotionally available scares us because what we know deep down inside is that means someone may call us on our *shit.* So the strong, quiet type is so attractive because they won't speak up and they won't say shit about us. We're going to always be right. Even when we're not right, they're going to *pacify* us by shutting the fuck up and letting us continue to do what we do. They just say, "Yes, baby, you right, you this, you that," which feels good, but we're not being confronted. And the challenge of emotionally available people is that *they* call us out in the same way that *we* call other people out. And so—because we may not feel like we're ready or we're not *accustomed* to dealing with people who're comfortable with confronting us or calling *us* out on our bullshit—we choose people that on a subconscious level we know won't be confronting or challenging for us.

But the *trade-off* for that is, when the rubber meets the road and you're in the *thick* of relationship challenges, that person won't know how to show up. Which is why, as we previously touched on, it is *so* important to question your type, and more importantly, to evaluate whether or not that person has the same level of emotional maturity as you—or has the *willingness* to grow beyond their current understanding.

I'm well out of my twenties now and let me tell you something: I *still* have to fight every goddamn instinct when a strong, quiet man over six one enters the room. I gotta stop myself from knocking somebody else over, smacking someone in the open, elbowing them in the face to get to him, because that is *my type*. It's not like that's ever gonna go away, but relationship after *relationship* has taught me that those guys don't *work* for me, and I have to respect that. It's worth not having that pain later on. You have to choose to *build* relationships with people—dating, romantic, and even professional—who show *clear* evidence that they are *as* emotionally mature as you.

In many cases, emotional unavailability is *simply* a symptom of the fact that that person has not worked through some things and is not emotionally mature in some areas. They have not *developed* the tools for communicating their feelings that are necessary to build truly healthy connections and relationships. They probably don't even *know* their feelings. I used to get all up in their face about this shit. I used to get so annoyed with them, like, *Why won't you tell me what you feel? Why won't you tell me?* Well, they don't fucking know! That's the answer. They don't *know*.

When he's sitting there staring at you looking like a goddamn *poodle* saying, "I don't know," he really doesn't fucking know! Maybe he was raised in an environment where he was put in a position to *suppress* his emotions rather than deal with them. It may not have been *safe* to confront his emotions. It is common for emotionally unavailable people to come from backgrounds where they've *dealt* with trauma—maybe they haven't learned to address their generational trauma and own their shit yet—and safety for them was in *not* processing or communicating their emotions.

It's gonna be tough to do, and this is coming from a guy who has to physically restrain himself from chatting up any tall, strong, silent man, but you gotta choose *not* to engage with them. You can send them prayers and well-wishes, but you can't build *relationships* of any remote level of intimacy with them because then *you* will be the person not getting your needs met, and it is a total *fucking* illusion to believe that you're going to be the person that's going to *help* them grow.

Now, before we move on to emotional unavailability within the context of family, we gotta step back and take a look at ourselves. Are *we* the emotionally unavailable ones? How can we tell? And if we *are*, how do we work through that?

It's *easy* to think of ourselves as emotionally available. For the longest time I always thought I was. I thought I'd *tell* you what I felt, so I *must* be emotionally available. Nuh-uh. Although I could voice *anger* and *disappointment* really well—at an expert level—I was not very good at being *vulnerable.* And that was one of the reasons why, in retrospect, I was so *afraid* to be in a relationship with someone who *was* actually emotionally available—because that person would ultimately hold me accountable in the areas where I wasn't emotionally available. That's why I chose all those strong, silent types who themselves weren't emotionally available. I was *choosing* the easy way out.

You can *tell* whether you're emotionally unavailable by doing one thing: asking three to five people who are actually close to you—or even just one person close to you—"On a scale from one to ten, ten being high, one being low, how vulnerable am I? How *open* do you feel I am about my feelings?"

When I did that, I got answers that changed my entire perception of myself. Those I asked said, "You're not very vulnerable. I know when you're angry, and I know when you're horny. But I don't know your feelings other than that."

To which I said, "Well, I feel good. I'm not really angry that often."

"Yeah, but that's the thing. Every time I ask you how you're doing, you say, 'Good, I'm great.' It's not very vulnerable because no one's *always* great."

That's the epitome of vulnerability—being able to share your true and honest feelings with others, even if it will open you up to scrutiny or judgment, even if it means you can't pretend to just be *doing great* all the time. And I tell you, I wasn't receptive to the idea. I fought it. I ignored it up until I couldn't—up until I realized that it was coming out in my parenting.

You know, there are times when my nephew-sons do something and I just get fucking *pissed*. I'm *literally* loud and *all* fucking wrong, and I'm cussing everybody out. And then I storm down the hall feeling like I made my point. But once I get to my room, it hits me. It hits me that I was just a total fucking asshole because *I* didn't acknowledge how *they* felt. I just attacked what they *did*. I wasn't vulnerable with them. I didn't acknowledge where *I* was wrong. I didn't notice how *I* played into this. And now I gotta apologize.

There is *nothing* worse than the feeling of knowing you gotta go back and set things right when you just blew your damn gasket. I've had to practice my apologies because I ain't come from a childhood where parents apologized to their kids. So I've had to learn how to do that on my own, how to give a real, heartfelt apology. How to stop at the apology and not include a qualifier like "but, however..." How to be comfortable expressing difficult intimate emotions to other people—including my kids. I'm *still* practicing that because there are still times that I get pissed and I don't feel like apologizing, but I *know* that I have to because they deserve that. And I know that withholding that from them is doing them wrong.

So, the key to measuring your own emotional availability is to ask the people who deal with you the *most*. Ask yourself, *When I hear the word "vulnerability," how does that make me feel?* Because those who struggle with vulnerability usually have a *visceral* reaction to the word. It's *scary*.

How open am I?

When I'm having a hard day, when I'm dealing with something that I'm ashamed of or embarrassed about, how willing am I to share that with someone else?

What's your reaction?

And if you really want to get froggy with it, ask yourself or those close to you, "When I'm wrong, how *often* do you feel that I apologize?" or, "How often do you feel like I take responsibility for my actions?" Don't ask the people who you know will give you the answer you want to hear, like your grandma who sees no wrong in you. Ask the people who you're close to, who've likely had disagreements with you in the past. How other people experience us can be very *telling* in terms of our own blind spots and internal shadows that we can't see. Asking is the *only* way we're ever going to know what they are and where we stand on emotional availability.

And if you've asked yourself those questions and you *are* emotionally unavailable, don't fret. Remember that it had to come from *somewhere*. In all likelihood, it stems from your formative years, perhaps from the generational trauma passed down through the family. It's *your* shit, and what have we said about that? *Own your shit*, then *change your shit*.

How were you parented? What pissed you off? And which behaviors of those are *you* carrying forward in your life? Remember the three steps to change: recognition, *choosing* to do different when you are triggered (*not* learning to not be triggered), and showing love instead of anger. Humanizing yourself and each other will go a *long* way toward creating empathy for everyone involved and through generations.

But relationships aren't the only place where we deal with emotionally unavailable people, and they usually aren't even the first place we see them. I *know* y'all know someone who is emotionally unavailable in your family, which again is *why* you might seek those types of people out in your relationships in the first place—you're attracted to what you already know, whether it's good or bad. We just don't realize how much what we see early on influences what we seek later. We learn to accept, and even be attracted to, emotionally unavailable people based on what happened during our formative relationships.

Say you have a pattern of being *unintentionally* attracted to emotionally unavailable people. You may find that some of those traits very much mirror the traits you saw in a mother, a father, or some other significant person in your formative years. And in the case of *family*, I know that can be a touchy subject. With an emotionally unavailable friend or someone else, someone who is *not* blood related, the minute you gain a little sense and realize your relationship with them may be toxic, you *know* you have an exit plan. You *know* you can get out of it. You are *aware* that you don't have to be in this. But with family? Family is different.

We often convince ourselves that "I just gotta deal with how Big Mama is. I just got to deal with how Dad is. I know she like this. I know he like this." Then we end up developing unhealthy coping mechanisms—not even just to cope, but to *tolerate* them—and, in a lot of cases, to actually work *with* them. *You* have to figure out the tools to keep allowing room in your life for that person or those people. Because *it's family*. You think, "I don't want to lose them." Y'all know the old saying: Blood is thicker than water. I get it. I ain't saying cut everyone off. In fact, it is *unhealthy* to just tell people to preemptively cut off relations, but *boundaries* are thicker than blood. With family, you have to have even *stronger* boundaries for how you deal with them, and the emotionally unavailable ones in particular, because how you deal with family will mirror how you deal with the rest of the world.

So where did you learn to tolerate emotionally unavailable relationships? Who within your close circle was that person to you? Who was your first experience with an emotionally unavailable person? And if that person is still in your life, what are the appropriate boundaries to put in place? It is so crucial to be willing to have those deep, honest conversations with yourself, or with a therapist, when it comes to family.

There are many ways emotional unavailability shows up in family, but if we're going with some of the most common, it often manifests itself in the form of someone who outright *ignores feelings*. Someone who can't give affection, whether that's in the form of hugs, kisses, or saying "I love you." Often it's a generational thing. I look at my aunts, all of them from that particular generation—and I don't want to pinpoint the women, but from my experience it's very heavy among a lot of Black women that I've grown up with, in my case particularly, Southern women. They're *very* loving in terms of the ability to be caregivers, to be your support system. If you ever go through *anything*, she got your back. But in terms of their ability to say "I love you," or in some cases to distribute hugs and be physically or verbally affectionate, they struggle with it. And *because* they struggle with it, there was a question in my mind as a little boy: *Do they love me?*

The newer generations are more *accustomed* to these outward expressions of affection, but the older generations aren't.

We've now normalized this behavior because we now understand that it's healthy, but older generations may not be able to give it because they probably never got it. Hell, they don't even do it for each other, so how they gonna do it for you? That's a question I had to come to terms with, and I'll put it in a nice little box for y'all: You can't get water from a well that's dry.

When you're dealing with *anyone* who lacks emotional availability in terms of their expressions of it, you need to step away. *Not* cut them off if you don't want to do that, but step away and recognize that you aren't getting, and probably won't *ever* get, that affection from them in the way you want. And that's *okay*. You can get it somewhere else. You just need to focus your energy on cultivating relationships with people who *can* give it to you, rather than waiting on that person to suddenly change into some whole different person and start acting the complete opposite of how they usually carry themselves. Now, does that even sound realistic? Then why've you been waiting on it? This person—your mother, your father, your grandparents, aunt, uncle, whoever—is not gonna change. You can try to force a hug on them, but it's going to be the most awkward hug on earth. You can say, "I love you," and they'll be like, "Yeah, okay." That half-hearted response is all you're gonna get because they just can't say it. So stop wasting your time.

Another common form of emotional unavailability in our formative years is the silent treatment or stonewalling. Now, just to be clear, these are the *same*. Tell everyone you know to Google it because it is a form of abuse, and it doesn't matter whether the person intended it to be or not. It *is* abuse because of the impact it has on the other person. It teaches them that when they do something you don't like or agree with, they become nonexistent to you until *you* decide they exist again within your life. That is an *incredibly* big act of emotional violence against someone. Take it from me because y'all now know that it was a common act of emotional violence in my own household growing up that made me traumatized and question my own self-worth—which then led to my people-pleasing behaviors that plagued me for years into my adulthood. So from that perspective, you need to accept that it is unacceptable. And while you cannot *change* the person who's choosing to do it, I recommend you let them *know* how it makes you feel. Sound familiar? Yes, we are *giving them your guidebook*. Not with the intention of changing them, but so that you can give them a heads-up as to why your *next* step—if they choose to continue ignoring your feelings—will be to distance yourself from them.

As we saw in previous chapters, the first step to dealing with someone who is not treating you the right way (in this case, giving you the silent treatment) is to be very clear with them about how it makes you feel.

"When you shut me out, when you don't talk to me for hours or days after we disagree, it makes me feel sad and unloved." Let them know how it impacts you and how it *may* impact your willingness to be close to them if it continues.

"It makes it very challenging for me to see being close to you in the future. It makes me shut down with you, and I no longer want to share even good news with you. It makes me not want to have a relationship with you. I'm telling you this because this is important to me, because our relationship is important."

Remember as you're formulating your words and thoughts that your primary goal is to negotiate a *compromise*. Sure, some people are vicious, and they just want to hurt others, but most aren't. Keep that in mind. Be empathetic. Some people give you the silent treatment simply because they don't know *how* to voice their feelings, and they need *time* to process them. Is that the case with your family member? If it is, maybe they really do need silence because maybe they have a background where, as a kid, if they voiced their opinion or feelings, that resulted in them getting popped by a parent. You don't always know, but you can find out. Because if they're not *choosing* to be this way and aren't shutting down just to hurt you, then it's on *you* to be understanding enough to realize that this is all they know *how* to do. So reach out. Offer that olive branch. "Hey, I want to find a middle ground that works for both of us."

With that understood, their behavior is not about you. What I do with people once I recognize the silent treatment is I'll say, "I want to give you time to think about what you're going to say, because hearing your feelings is very important to me. Because that's something that helps our relationship. So when we're talking, can you make this agreement with me? If I make the agreement to respect the fact that you need a little time to think about what you feel, can *you* make the agreement that in those moments, you will *tell* me, 'I need time to think about what I feel'? And then give me a time for when we can come back together to finish the conversation? Can we come back together in an hour? Can we come back together tomorrow? So you will *voice* to me that you're not ready to talk, but you will also give me a very *clear* time for when I can expect that we will talk."

I've done this as a parent, as a partner, and generally speaking, this encouragement will allow the other person to recognize the pattern for themselves and catch on. It is *incredibly* helpful. Yes, you're initially going to have to remind them when they *do* go silent and give them a little nudge, like, "Hey, is this one of the moments where you need time to think about what you're feeling? Can we talk again after dinner? Great." You may have to do that on and off until they catch on. But if that person *desires* to be in a healthy relationship like you, then you'll find they *will* do it. They just don't have the tools to do it on their own yet. The fact that *you're* reading this book means you've gone looking for such tools and probably have some already. They don't have that. So it's important to recognize you may be a bit more advanced than the people you're dealing with in terms of emotional availability and be willing to help them *facilitate* the process of moving forward in this direction.

Once you've identified where in your life you first dealt with tolerating and accepting emotional unavailability, then we can talk about some boundaries to anchor in place when it comes to family.

Number one: *Do not go to a dry well.*

Remember the water well? If it's dry, stop going. If you have an emotionally unavailable family member who doesn't respond to you coaching them on expressing their feelings and who still can't give you the level of emotional availability you need—whether it's accountability, feedback, support, empathy—when you're going through something, *stop fucking going to them.* I do not care how close this family member is to you. They don't need to get your good news. They don't need to hear about your bad day. They don't need to hear what you feel.

Years ago, I was with this therapist who, *culturally*, did not have a very clear understanding of the dynamics of where I came from: Southern Black culture. I was venting in my sessions, saying that such-and-such person wasn't giving me this or giving me what I wanted, and she just kept repeating the same old thing.

"Just *tell* your family member how you *feel* about them."

I said, "Do you understand I've tried this for the last thirty fucking years? And it is an abusive experience to tell them because they will *always* turn it back around on me."

She responded with "You have to keep telling them and holding them accountable."

Lady, no. That's going to the same fucking dry well over and over when nothing is there. But she just didn't get that. She didn't understand. And it wasn't until I went to a different therapist who was more culturally astute in the dynamics of Southern Black culture that I got the advice I needed. When I rehashed everything to her, she took a completely different tack.

"You can love that family member but *stop* going to them and telling them the same thing and *expecting* different results. This person loves you, but you got to learn to deal with them differently."

If we keep voluntarily going to the same emotionally unavailable people and expecting them to magically change, then we're the ones now inviting their treatment toward us. Because we *keep going to them* with our news. We keep giving them access to certain parts of our lives that they don't need! And we expect something different to happen each time, which is just plain foolish.

This leads us to **number two:** ***Be selective.***

Everyone is not entitled to every part of you, *especially* family. The only thing family got in common is that, genetically, y'all got some shared DNA. They are *not* entitled to any greater access to you or any greater information than anyone else. They have to live by and treat you by the same damn rules of respect that you would expect of anyone else. Family *needs* strong boundaries. We have to get out of this mindset that just because someone is a family member they deserve access to us. That is *not* true.

If you're having a tough time dealing with what to say, honey, I got you. Let me tell you about this conversation I had when I was having a tough day. One of my nephews wanted to have a birthday dinner, and I was not about it. But I took everybody out because I wasn't gonna sit home. Their lives still deserve to be celebrated and enjoyed, and that shouldn't stop just because I'm having a bad day. So, we went.

When we get there, there's a big group at the table. I'm sitting there, clearly stressed, on my phone, dealing with the work matters at hand. Going, going, going. I'm not invested in what's happening around me. Fortunately, my nephew understood what was going on already. He was not taking it personally. *However*, there was another family member at the table who is *notoriously* emotionally unavailable—her form of emotional unavailability shows through in her *ignoring* how I feel and the clear signs and symptoms of what's going on.

So, I'm sitting there on my phone, texting or whatever, and I'm talking occasionally, and she just leans in and goes, "You need to pay attention. It's a birthday dinner going on here. What're you so stressed-out about?"

You know, telling me I just need to lighten up. *Ignoring* how I was feeling. So, in that moment, I had to set down very strong boundaries. It wasn't for me. I love this person in my family. This family member is also from a much older generation, so I'm not expecting to change her. I gently put my hand on her lap—I'm being nice about it because you know my words are gonna be strong—and I set my boundary.

I said, "I'm currently focused on something that is eliminating my ability to focus on anything other than what I need to be focused on right now. I know that you would like my attention.

However, you are ignoring the fact that I'm not able to give that to you right now. There are other people at the table. You should talk to them if I'm not giving you the kind of reaction that you want."

And she goes, "Whatever. I'm going to keep on talking to you anyway."

Oh, so that's how it's gonna go? Well, my boundary ain't shifting because of your nasty attitude. So, I respond, "Then I'm going to get up and move chairs because I'm not going to focus my energy on anything other than what I want to focus my energy on right now, which is this matter at hand. And this has nothing to do with you."

In the past, I probably would have resigned myself to having to talk to her all damn night. I would've let her deal with me in different kinds of ways. That's the tricky thing about family. You have to be very clear with them about setting boundaries because it ain't something they're gonna be used to. They're used to being given license in the past. They're used to you *accepting* some of their bullshit. Of course they ain't gonna want to change! They want that open-door policy, and you're actively trying to shut one of them. So there will be tension. But there doesn't have to be rage or rudeness. Set a boundary that is not *mean*, not *accusatory*, but just very clear: "This is the road that you can go down, and it's the *only* road you can go down with me. You have no other option."

And just like with those who give you the silent treatment, it's gonna be a process. You are going to have to *repeatedly* set your boundaries and your intentions around each emotionally unavailable person because now you've learned and changed your mind about how they can treat you, and they're not used to that yet. Just realize that you may have to rinse and repeat more often with them than with someone you don't have quite as much history with.

When it comes to dealing with the emotionally unavailable, we like to simplify. We tell others to just leave the toxic relationship or to just cut off that family member that drives them up the wall because they're not getting the right response from them. We tell them all these things or we *get* told these things to avoid pain.

We cannot *avoid* pain. Oftentimes we think we're avoiding pain by keeping a toxic relationship because we don't want to go through the pain of cutting off this family member or ending this relationship or friendship with someone who's emotionally unavailable. We don't want to have to deal with what they'll say or how they'll feel. So we abuse *ourselves*. That's what we do when we stay in these relationships or friendships in order to maintain one with *anybody* who *consistently* is proving to you that they are unable—but more importantly, *unwilling*—to make the changes to be able to be a healthy contributor to your life.

This doesn't mean that trying to change should be a perfect experience or that they will become perfect people, but they at least need to be a *healthy* contributor to your life. And so when it comes to cutting people off, it comes down to this: You have to love yourself enough to be *willing* to experience the pain of letting go of a relationship that is not *loving* for you. If you don't, and you continue to exist in this hurtful sphere of emotional unavailability, all you're doing is creating *inevitable* long-term pain for *yourself.*

The pain of letting go of a toxic relationship opens the door to your own internal *power.* It's you saying no to people who will mistreat you. That pain you may experience in doing so is just the clearing of space in your life for someone who *can* fill that space in a healthy way. But as long as you keep staying in that toxic relationship, the pain will be perpetual. It will keep on going on and on. And worse, that person will continue to show you new and more profound ways of hurting you as you continue giving *them* that power to do so.

So how do you leave?

I always tell people that if they're not ready to leave that toxic relationship, then don't. You'll be ready eventually. Or the situation will get so bad you'll *have* to leave. Do I want it to come to that point? Hell no. But the person *in* that relationship is the only one who can change anything about it. So consider this if you're in this position: *If you wait until you're "ready," whenever that time may be, what will be the consequence? What damage will you have done to yourself?*

So think about what it's going to cost you once you get to that point. Think about the saying "Tomorrow is not promised and today is not a guarantee, either." So how much energy do you want to continue to put into something that is *clearly* dead?

There's no magic bullet for instructing people on how to leave an unhealthy relationship. We all have that choice at any time. The choice is between bitter and better, and, honey, I decided I was gonna get *better*. I needed relationships around me that could be *there* for me and that I could be there for, too. I needed healthy relationships, and there ain't *nothing* healthy about someone who doesn't show up for you emotionally. What it comes down to is asking yourself, *Do I deserve to live a life in which this pain is no longer a part of it?*

Take Action to Get the F*ck Out Your Own Way

Based on your answers to the questions posed in this chapter, are you emotionally unavailable? If you are, go back to chapters 1 and 2 and walk through the steps to work through your shit. Understand your triggers and deal with that pain in a productive way. Ask yourself how you've been parented and how that handed-down trauma may be manifesting itself in your current behavior.

Set CLEAR boundaries for your family. Vocalize when they're giving you the silent treatment and know when to stop visiting a well that's already dry. They're your family, but that ain't gotta mean you have to be an open book. Be selective about what parts of your life they are allowed to know.

If you're in a toxic relationship or friendship, don't avoid the pain. Ask yourself what the consequences will be if you don't leave—how will you be hurt?

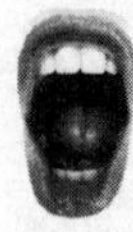

8

Do You Even *Want* a Relationship, or Do You Just *Think* You Do?

So far we've discussed what to do when you're in, or almost in, a relationship that is not serving you, but we haven't gotten to the question that it begs: How did we even get into those relationships in the *first* place? What choices did we make that led to this, and how can we stop making those same fucked-up choices? I bet you were thinking, *Well, now, how can I get around all this? How can I prevent any of this from happening at all?*

Honey, great question.

My mantra is *Don't make choices when you're horny, hungry, or lonely.*

The thing is, that's when most of us *do* make choices—when we're feeling in need of something or starved for something. Like choosing a partner when you're lonely is a shortcut to getting rid of loneliness—like it's gonna speed up the process. But it doesn't work that way. What it does is it just preys on our already-fragile mentalities. It lowers our ability to hear our inner voice. It creates a *competing* voice. And when those competing voices get loud, it's hard to make a distinction between what we really need and what we're *hearing* we need.

These voices ain't easy to ignore. There were a lot of times in my life when I was definitely way more sexual than I needed to be. I may have *felt* good during the act, but afterward I'd be sitting there and thinking, *This isn't really what I want.* The minute the act was over, I was over him. Because I didn't want him. I wanted to feel desired, like we talked about before. *That's* what my inner voice was saying, but I couldn't hear the other voices that were saying, "I wanna feel desired. I want to feel nurtured. I want someone to be here. I don't want to be here by myself."

What you gotta realize is that these competing voices, while real, are also topical. They are *always* connected to a deeper, underlying need. It's like anger. Anger is an emotion that always connects to something else. No one is just angry. What they really are is hurt. They're lonely, afraid, or anxious, and it's *coming out* in the form of anger. It's the same thing here. Let's take a closer look at loneliness.

Loneliness is a self-inflicted emotion just like shame—and I say self-inflicted not because you choose to be lonely but from the point of view that we have the tools to fix it on our own and we often choose not to. Loneliness is actually *not* something that can be fixed by someone else. Therefore, to continue feeling that way is on you. Loneliness isn't always fixed by having someone around anyway. Hell, you can be in a crowded room and still feel lonely even though there's people all around you.

So what do *you* want?

That's the question you should be asking yourself. *What do I really want out of this person being here?*

Maybe it's someone you can talk to about whatever you're going through. Or someone you wish you could cuddle or have sex with. What is your *root* need that's being unmet? Once you have that nailed down, then it's a matter of going out and finding how you can get this need met, even if it's not within the context of a relationship. Maybe it's in a piecemeal way. I go to this friend for this, this person for that, and so on. What you'll realize very quickly, once you start having those needs met, is that you're not lonely anymore. *That's* how you fix your own loneliness, rather than investing time in a potential partner who ain't what you're really looking for just to keep the loneliness away. You don't have to try to get all your needs met through one person.

The presence of other human beings doesn't fix loneliness. All it does is give you someone else to have around, and even then you may still feel lonely. This is why we have to take a step back and ask ourselves what we want, who we want, and *if* we even want a relationship or not. Because believe it or not, oftentimes our needs are disguised as a desire to be with someone else.

"I want to be in a relationship." No, what you're looking for is financial security because life is tough paying bills on your own.

"I really want to be with someone." No, what you really want is a readily available emotional support system.

"I really want somebody." No, what you want is consistent sex, *but* it's been culturally ingrained in you that you're a bad girl or a bad boy for wanting sex outside the context of a relationship.

So how do you know when you're making a bad choice based on loneliness? Check in with yourself. Write down the things you want. You can even think of it as the characteristics you want in a spouse. *I want this, I want that.* And after you've done that, ask yourself if there's a way to get each of those traits *without* being in a relationship. Maybe you really want companionship and someone to do things with because you love to travel. A relationship *could* provide that, but having a travel buddy—just a responsible, mature adult who desires the same thing—can, too.

I ain't saying to put a relationship off *completely*. But I *am* saying that it's two separate things: the thing you want and a relationship. What you want doesn't *have* to wait until you're *in* a relationship. If you want somebody to reach out to, a support system, then maybe it's time for you to cultivate the friendships in your life that could provide that. Maybe sex won't come with that support system, but you do have that other friend, that person who maybe it'd be a great time to rekindle with. Now, if a relationship *comes* with those things, then that's great. But you shouldn't put all the pressure to fill those needs on a relationship because that's how you're gonna end up in ones that do not serve you.

When you desire to have a relationship or someone in your life just because you want someone there and it's *not* about having specific qualities in that person, that's a red flag—not only should it be a red flag to them but it should be a red flag to *you* as well because that means that the desire to just have *something* to fill the space in your life is *more* prominent than your consideration of whether the actual traits that person has will match up with your own. That's when you end up going the wrong way. When you find yourself saying in minute ways, *I don't want you here. I just want a warm body until I get what I need.* You just desire the presence of somebody rather than their actual characteristics. Because when you truly desire a *relationship*, not just a body, you'll be all over those characteristics.

I would love to have someone that I can talk about great books with, with whom I can read. I would love to have someone with whom I can travel. Someone who values family and I can have a family with. Those are added *qualities.* And remember, some of them you may get through friends. But if you're just focused on someone's presence, that's a good indication that what you're really trying to address is loneliness. So taking inventory of ourselves is one of the most helpful things we can do, and what's more is *it ain't hard.* We don't do it not because it's hard but because we ain't built up those habits. But if you *can* be intentional about how you feel and the choices you make, then it can help a lot.

For me and for what I'm guessing is a large percentage of y'all, we grew up with the expectation of being married stamped on our goddamn foreheads. It's like we were born with a tag that says, *You will get married one day*. Even my mother said, "I don't care if you're gay or not. You're gonna get married." It was a bottom line, no argument. In my family, people were married with kids by the age of twenty-one. And even that was late. That's just how we were. There was this cultural expectation put on me that a relationship was the one thing I *needed*, the one thing that was going to *provide* for and *meet* every one of my needs. So I played to that all in my twenties. I was a serial monogamist. I jumped from relationship to relationship, and in between relationships, I threw this ass in a *circle* from coast to coast looking for my man. And I still haven't found him. But what I *did* find, thanks to the pandemic, were other ways to fill my needs *independent* of a relationship. It wasn't me giving up on looking for relationships; I *had* to find other ways, and even though I'd had an inkling that searching for a relationship wasn't the best way to meet my needs before, the pandemic was really what cemented that for me. You know, I wasn't fucking during those months, but I got the world's best vibrator collection. Boom, need met. What about the others? That's how I beat this habit.

So when I finally began to fill my needs in other ways, I realized that I didn't desire a relationship—or at least I didn't desire one with the same burning feeling as before. Before, I felt like I was deficient without a relationship. But I ain't deficient. I have my needs met now. So while, before, I was using a relationship to meet a need, now I have the understanding that my next relationship is only going to *complement* what I already have. And that will make me a *far* better person to be in a relationship with once I go back to dating.

But I ain't chasing.

I ain't doing all that because now I'm not looking for a man to fill that void. I could take it or leave it.

Years ago I met with this relationship coach and filmed it for one of my videos. And let me tell you, this woman showed me exactly how far I'd grown and changed in this regard—and I don't think she even meant to!

She came to my house to film and I thought, *Oh we're just filming this for content.* But she was doing a *real* evaluation for which I was not fucking prepared! She was assessing whether or not I was even ready for a relationship, since I give all these relationship talks.

Her first stop was the bathroom and she goes, "See, you're not ready."

I'm looking around the space and it looks fine. I got no idea what she's on about, so I go, "Why?"

"You take up the whole space," she said.

"I need a space to brush my teeth and I need my makeup side. I don't want to be brushing my teeth on the makeup side. It's different activities."

She was *unimpressed.* She says, "You have to create room for a man. Like your closet. You take up the whole closet. You're gonna have to work a lot less to create room for a man."

It was like that the whole damn tour. She goes from room to room telling me all these things I need to do different to make room for a man.

And the whole time I'm thinking to myself, *Well, shit, I want a man, but I don't want the kind you're talking about!* The kind of man I'm talking about is like, "Shit, let's go buy a bigger house." That's what I *want.* I don't want a man that I gotta take care of, I don't want to have to take care of nobody because I was already getting that need fulfilled. I got kids, and I take care of them all the damn time. Beforehand I would've *jumped* at everything this woman was saying because of my desire to feel needed. I would've moved heaven and earth to take care of somebody. But not anymore. My needs have been met, which means I now have the power to say, *This is what I really want. And I ain't gonna settle for anything less.*

Having your needs met *will* change the definition of what you want. It might mean a change in what you want in a partner or whether you want a relationship at all. If you can find ways to get the needs that you once wanted in a relationship met, and you *still* want a relationship, then it sounds like companionship is for you. But if you find a way to get all your needs met through this, you may find that the type of relationship that you *thought* you wanted is not actually the type of relationship you want, period.

Once you become the healthy, fulfilled, and full person you are, your position in the world of dating *will* shift, including the type of person you're looking for—*if* you decide you truly want a relationship. You ain't just a reflection of your unmet needs—you are whole. And that person requires a different partner; hell, they might not even *require* a partner. Maybe just a companion.

But that's up to you to figure out.

Take Action to Get the F*ck Out Your Own Way

Take a step back. What are you searching for–qualities or just a warm body? Ask yourself what unmet needs you have and how you can fulfill them. You may find that once they're met, what you want changes–including wanting a relationship at all.

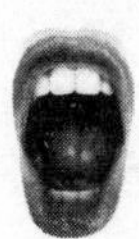

9

Embracing Your Masculine and Feminine Energies + My Partner's Sexual Orientation—Examining Our Biases

We've talked a lot so far about relationships and if we even *want* one, but let's say you're in one or you *do* want one. Even if you *don't* want one, the advice you'll hear in this chapter will help—for any kind of relationship or friendship. But most importantly, for *you*.

As a society, we *love* to talk about masculinity and femininity. I *honestly* do not understand the big deal, but we love to put anything we can into gendered boxes. Even with the recent discussions about gender fluidity and pronouns, we *still* gender the *hell* out of things. But what I never hear enough about is masculine and feminine *energy*, and how *integral* they are, not just to individual people, but to our relationships and our communities. So, you bet, sis, we are gonna talk about them *now*. Get in here!

Feminine energy comes from feeling comfortable being in the *flow* of things. It is *not* trying to lead, direct, or dictate control, and it is *not* the same as weak or submissive energy, but it *is* more passive than masculine energy. Too many folks out there think feminine energy is synonymous with "submissive." And that's just fucking wrong. I know *a lot* of feminine women who are not *weak*. Feminine energy is being *confident* in your ability to *influence* the outcomes that you desire. And *because* of your confidence in your ability to influence outcomes that you desire, you do not *lean* into trying to *control* and *dictate* the outcomes. *That's* feeling comfortable in the flow of things.

Feminine energy is the *most* powerful energy because it strengthens *influence* and *intuition*—the things that can't be seen or felt. Y'all familiar with that movie *My Big Fat Greek Wedding*? They have one of the best analogies for this: Masculine energy is the head. Feminine energy is the *neck*—and the neck can make the head turn however it wants it to. That energy, ultimately, is leading and *guiding* everything. And it, to *me*, is when we are most in control of ourselves because we are not *forcing* anything, like we do when we are operating within our masculine energy.

Masculine energy is *decisive*. And don't get me wrong, that can be good, too, because sometimes you *have* to be decisive. But the problem is, we got way too many people out here *only* operating in their masculine energy. And when you *only* harness that energy, rather than balance it with your feminine energy, it often becomes about *pushing* for the outcomes that you want. It is *chasing*. Masculine energy is gonna chase you down; it is going to *get* what it wants through *any* means.

I'm gonna *force* it.

I'm gonna *push* it.

I'm gonna try to *dominate* it.

I need to be in *control* in the most *visible* way possible.

You know what this screams to me? Insecurity. Masculine energy can lead to *insecurity*. Because if I *truly* have power, why do I have to make sure that everybody knows?

If I truly know that what I want *wants* me, why would I have to chase it? Why would I have to convince it?

If you only operate within your masculine energy, you're only operating in the most insecure parts of yourself. And if you only operate within your feminine energy, you're only operating in the most passive parts of yourself. Y'all see the dilemma? You can't have one without the other. Masculine energy *needs* feminine energy because it is a *stabilizing* force. It helps harness masculine energy so that it can actually be used in a way that's going to be *helpful*, that's going to be *constructive* rather than *destructive.*

When you tie those energies together, you're *using* your assertiveness. You're using your ability to produce outcomes, and you're tying it to a level of *ease* and a level of *influence* that doesn't *require* you to exhaust yourself to get that outcome. You're *balancing* your energies, which too many of you think is fucking impossible.

It ain't.

True power is your masculine and feminine energies working together. And that true power doesn't have to force anything. It simply goes in the direction that it *needs* to go in based on what's best for that moment.

When I tell people my power comes from *enjoying* and *embracing* my femininity but *also* embracing my masculinity, I see so many eyes rolling. You know what they tell me? "That's easy for *you*. You a gay man. So of course you have both."

Well you got both, too.

You just haven't *done* anything about them. And most of y'all in relationships *definitely* don't know you have both. How many times have you asked or heard someone ask, "How can I be more feminine for my man? How can I be more masculine?"

Honey, that question only comes up when you've chosen the *wrong* person.

And *that* comes when we don't know our *own* energies in the first place.

Not knowing or understanding our own energies is a goddamn tragedy born straight from the fact that we haven't *properly* assessed our own energies as a culture *and* as individuals. We need to stop asking, *How can you be more feminine or masculine?* That's the *wrong* question. Instead of asking how you can *fix* your energies, you should be asking if you are *comfortable* in each one.

For most of my life, I operated heavily within my feminine energy. I was *always* very passive. Always comfortable allowing other people to lead and guide, always comfortable with being a *nurturer*, a *supporter*, and it did me wrong in so many ways. It led me into relationships that didn't *serve* me. Into spaces where I would *suffer* over and over again because I didn't speak up or step up. I was overrun by that forceful masculine energy. In those situations, the consequences that I *knew* were gonna happen ended up happening—he'd cheat, he'd be abusive, he'd lie—and I didn't do a damn thing about it because I was leaning too far into my feminine energy and being *too passive*. That led to me getting taken advantage of. My feelings were always on my sleeve, which made me a target for treatment that I frankly just didn't desire or deserve. But I didn't think I *could* change any of that. Not until I learned to harness *both* my masculine and my feminine energies.

Let's get real. Forget about your man, woman, or whoever for a minute. Look at yourself. Do you operate more within your feminine or masculine energy? Are you *comfortable* with your less dominant energy?

No, you ain't. The *majority* of people ain't.

The reason we aren't comfortable is because we don't assess our energies according to who *we* are, but rather according to what we *think* we should be, or what we believe *society* wants us to be.

Let's talk about women for a minute, specifically *heterosexual, feminine-presenting* women. The reality is that a *significant* number of these women have significant *masculine* traits, and that's *okay*. Yes, honey. Yes, darling, *it is okay*. Society may never have told you that, your parents may never have told you that, but I got your back, baby, because I *was* you.

You have moments where you *know* you gotta speak up. You *gotta* stand up. You *know* the outcome would be better if you just tapped *into* your masculine energy, but you're hesitant to.

That's not me, you think to yourself.

The sooner you embrace that shit and let it *help* you in your life, the *better*. Because here's the thing you gotta realize: Our energies do not just sit passively within us. Whether it's your masculine or feminine energy being held back, it *will* come out. That energy *will* show itself. We might try to keep forcing it back down because it doesn't fit within the image of what we think we *should* be, though. I learned to become *selective* of where I would let my masculine energy come out. It could come out in business. When it did, it produced *wonderful* outcomes—oh, my goodness, taking charge and getting shit *done*, honey! But then, when I got home to my boyfriend, I'd cut that shit off.

And you know what?

You *can't* cut that off.

Once you start to taste the sweetness of what that masculine energy can get you in life—ooh, *baby*, it's a beautiful thing. So, when me and mine would get in an argument, a nasty ol' argument where the next thing I know is whoopsie, I'm showing him an energy source he's never seen before, and now it's a *power* struggle. He's answering *my* masculine energy with his own, and with both of us trying to take control, ain't neither one of us gonna end up having it. He wasn't used to that masculine energy from me, so it created that power struggle. If I'd chosen someone who was *also* centered in *their* masculine and feminine energies, both, then we would have been more equally yoked when I was finally able to step into my own power.

Understanding our energies and choosing our partners is a lot like going to the pharmacy: If you're not honest with yourself, or not *aware* of your diagnosis, then how can you pick the right solution, the right partner, for your body and for your life?

You can't.

You're gonna pick the wrong one.

You're looking for *opposites*, for this or for that, when you *should* be looking for a partner whose energy *complements* your own. That's why it is so, *so* important to be honest with *yourself* before choosing your partnerships and your friendships. It saves *you* trouble, and it saves *them* trouble. Because—and let me be frank about it—*you* are being unfair to *them*. It is *unfair* to build relationships with people without letting them see your full self. You are *letting* them make a mental agreement to be in a relationship with one thing, *one* energy. And later, when—not if, *when*—they see the other side of you, *when* they *reject* it, when they *push* against it, when they're *confused* and don't know what to do with it, that's when you turn the tables and *vilify* them.

Baby girl, ain't *none* of that fair.

It is *critical* for any *healthy*, *long-term* relationship—I don't care if it's business, platonic, romantic, regardless of the realm—that you show people your full self as *early* and as *often* as possible, so that people can make an informed decision about whether that's what *they're* comfortable with. But *also* so that you've given them permission to do the same thing, and that's how you're gonna find and have an authentic connection. But you can't do that if you're not open and honest with yourself about who you really are.

I *know* how difficult it is to look within yourself and see your own relationship with your masculine and feminine energies. Oftentimes we are *conditioned* to believe a certain thing about ourselves. You meet me, and right off the bat, you see I'm *physically* a pretty small person. I came out of the *womb* pretty, honey. My eyebrows are naturally arched, my booty is nice and high. I was not *built* to stand up here working on nobody's construction site. So, in my younger years I'd look at who I was, and I said, "This is what I'm built to be. This is who I am." So I'd *flaunt* my femininity. Shy *away* from my masculinity—unless the situation was picture-perfect for it, and even then, I kept it on a short leash to stay within the image of who I *thought* I was.

Ladies, I am speaking *directly* to you now. Let's start with biases about *ourselves.* Y'all know my story—feminine presenting all the time. I use myself as an example, but if we're getting down and dirty with the truth, y'all have it *far* worse, particularly women of color. The level of *pressure* around you to believe that just *because* you are a woman you are *supposed* to be feminine is fucking *unbelievable.* Being told you're supposed to be a certain way, like you're supposed to shut up when you're really the type to speak up? That expectation creates *a lot* of cognitive dissonance and turmoil. It is *traumatic.*

Being told, "You need to be more feminine," when the *truth* of the matter is that there are *many* parts of your life when you have *had* to be masculine, y'all may come to believe that your masculine traits are something you need to get *rid* of. But maybe, in your household, you *had* to take on a more masculine role to keep things going, maybe to protect siblings and take care of parents and stuff like that. You had a role based *in* your masculine energy. You were *rewarded* for being masculine within the context of your family. I hear women say all the time: "I wouldn't have to be this way if I didn't go through this fight or struggle. This shit *made* me like this," putting it out there like your masculine energy was born as the *result* of some hardship, and that just ain't true. I ain't saying you *didn't* go through some hardship, maybe you did, but whatever that was did not *create* this masculine energy.

Sweetie, you were *born* with it.

You *always* had it. At the end of the day, *no one* has all of just one energy. But we often access one side more than the other, some of us to a very extreme level that can cause us to *think* we ain't got none of the other. But we do. That other side is still in there and it needs to come out in order for you to find balance, especially now that you're on this healing journey that I know you're on because you're reading this book.

Denying one of our energies just makes us *ashamed* of that less-dominant energy. I *knew* my masculine energy was there; it was just suppressed. I was ashamed for it to come out. I didn't think it *should* come out, not unless I really, *really* wanted it to. Same for you, honey.

So, let's nip that shit in the bud. I encourage y'all women—and men, but *especially* women—to *accept* your masculine energy. Understand that just because you *have* it, just because you are *good* at being direct, does not make you any *less* of a woman. Just know that you have to be able to have equal control of *both* of your energies. And if a *man* can't deal with the masculine aspects of your energy, then that is *his* fucking problem. That just means he can't deal with his *own* feminine energy. That is *not* your problem, and do not *let* him *make* it your problem. This is the reason why there are a whole lot of women right now sitting in abusive relationships, getting their behinds beat because they have both energies and *a lot* of insecure-ass men can't *deal* with both of those energies coming out.

I'm here to tell you—hand on my heart, and swear on everything—that you *have* to accept both energies. It is *dangerous* not to. It can lead you to people who *also* won't accept your energy, which leads to them trying to *suppress* that energy in you, physically or verbally. Either way, it can become *abusive* and *unhealthy* for your mind and for your body.

The fact that most of us *don't* know our own levels of masculine and feminine energy is concerning not only for the individual and their relationships but for our *community*, too. *Especially* minority communities, *in particular* Black communities. Not having a *healthy* understanding of where we sit in our masculine and feminine energies—and not knowing others', either—leads to biases about *our* sexual orientation *and* that of our partners.

I'm calling it like I see it, and we're gonna dive into that next.

***

Thinking we're all just feminine or masculine not only creates turbulence within ourselves but also makes it *easier* for us to then be biased against our own *partners*. It happens, and it happens *often*. I've *seen* it. The sheer *number* of messages I've been sent along these lines, mostly from Black women, is just astounding. Hitting me up all outraged: *MJ, I found a video of my man with another man from twenty years ago. Does this mean he's gay?*

Honey, I *understand* why a video like that would concern you. But listen. That shit was *twenty* years ago! Why are you digging it up now and whooping all over it? We *all* have attractions that go *beyond* the scope of what our partner's physical identity is. So no, your man *isn't* suddenly gay or bi because you saw this and that on his Instagram or because he did this *one* sexual act twenty-something years ago! Stop focusing on what makes men's dicks hard and focus on whether or not he's *faithful* to you.

We jump to conclusions based on *unexamined biases* that come from the act of ignoring our own masculine and feminine energies. If y'all had *understood* and *accepted* that feminine energy within your man, this shit might've not turned into a fucking mountain. So the next time this happens, look *beyond* the genitals before you dump their ass. Understand your own energies and what you're looking for in your partner's energies. *Because*, in my unique position as someone whose videos cater *mainly* to women looking for relationship help, y'all are some of the *biggest* promoters of toxic masculinity.

Getting all riled up over a decades-old video in which your man displayed just a smidge of feminine energy? Thinking he's now gay? Bi? Dumping him at the drop of a hat because of that?

That is *toxic masculinity*. And *you're* promoting it by doing that.

A few other examples include telling boys to "man up" when they feel upset or justifying abusive and inappropriate behavior with the phrase "boys will be boys"—and don't that sound like what y'all encourage in your men's everyday behavior, then get mad when it starts to affect *you* negatively?

I'm gonna share a story with y'all, come on in. Y'all know I like to look good and dress up. Men gotta look good, too. I have made both my nephew-sons get manicures and pedicures since before high school. I always say to them, "You not gonna be walking around here with ugly hands and ugly feet. I don't care if you wearing socks twenty-four seven. You need to know how to make your shit look right and take care of yourself."

They both *love* it. Who *wouldn't* love a little pampering and self-care? One day, one of my nephew-sons says, "I want to get a design on one of my fingers." He wanted to get a money sign. Then he goes, "What you think people gonna say about it?"

I said, "It don't matter what they're going to say if that's what you want."

Hallelujah, he's off to the races. Couple weeks later, my other nephew-son comes and says, "I'm gonna get all my nails black."

He gets a few designs, and they look real nice. So I posted both of their videos to social media to celebrate what they'd done.

Baby, you would not *believe* the number of women—Black women—who wrote to me! It wasn't Black men, it was Black *women*, writing to me saying shit like "It's one thing to get a manicure, but color! Are you *sure* your nephews are straight?"

My nephew-sons are two straight men, *very* straight. And if they were gay, that'd be fine, too, but they *happen* to be straight. But not to these women. The *minute* they saw that feminine energy peeking out, it threatened their own assessment of who *they* were and what *others* could and should be, and they had to step on it because it didn't allow them to continue living in *their* limitations.

And you know what *occurred* to me when the floodgates opened?

That's why a lot of these women are sitting here single as *hell.*

Because the fact of the matter *is,* men don't feel safe being with them!

One of the things that keep some men from feeling safe enough with a woman to commit to her is that he doesn't feel like he can be his full self. You could have the most hyper-heterosexual man out there who likes nothing else other than women. However, he may like giving attention to grooming. He may be expressive about his emotions in some way, shape, or form. He may do things that could be referred to as feminine but that in no way compromise his sexual orientation. And one of the things I *know* to be true is that a man only chooses a woman that he feels *safe* with. He only sticks with a woman *long term* that he feels safe being his *full* self with. So if your beliefs about femininity and masculinity come out in a way that makes men feel unsafe, then you have to be aware that you could be pushing away really good men who are capable of loving you holistically.

We've also created this double-edged sword within our communities because men are conditioned to *accept* women's masculinity in a lot of cases, especially that of Black women, because she can run this show. She's been raised to do anything and everything, so the Black man knows she *can* run the show. She can be as feminine as she wants to be, but he's supposed to support *her* masculine energy when she has it. But we don't give that same grace to men. We have to give men the *same* grace to be accepted holistically.

We *love* to talk about toxic masculinity, but what we don't acknowledge is that some of its biggest promoters are *women* who don't want to *accept* the polarity of the fact that people have a *balance* of energies and that someone's *willingness* to do things that we might traditionally think of as feminine doesn't make them less of a man! Just like a *woman* doing something that may present as more masculine doesn't make her any less of a woman—mm-hmm, remember that whole conversation we just had about y'all having masculine energy and it's okay? Well, it's okay that *he* has a balance of energies as well. And, unfortunately, that really does create a lot of *conflict* and *turmoil* within our communities, this double standard that's at play.

A narrow-minded perspective on sexual orientation only adds more fuel to the fire when it comes to our understanding of gender roles within our communities. There are a whole lot of women out here who could really *rule* the world if they *leaned* into their masculine energy. Could be *rewarded* with so many great things. Instead, they're living lives so far *less* than what they desire and what they deserve because they're *afraid* of being viewed as a lesbian or too masculine. They're afraid of being viewed as too *hard*, or whatever it may be, if those traits come out.

And you got a whole lot of *men* out here who are *literally* operating in roles they're not qualified to be in within in their household for this same reason—trying to lead and direct a household, just because *society* says they should, when they can't even lead and direct their way out of a fucking paper *bag*. You see what I'm saying? Those types of men are beta males, and there ain't nothing wrong with that! They *need* to be with a woman who's more masculine, and yet they're *afraid* to accept the fact that they are betas. They're *afraid* to say, "Well, I'm more passive. I *like* when she makes decisions. I *appreciate* that shit." No, he's afraid of saying that because he's afraid of being called *gay* or whatever it may be, so now he's stuck operating in roles he's not qualified to do, and *everybody* is suffering. The household is suffering because shit ain't getting done, and he's suffering because he's living in fear and insecurity trying to play a role that he has no idea how to properly execute. I'm sure we all know a man like this. Well, this is why he's like that.

Then on the *flip* side, I know a whole lot of *masculine-ass gay men*, too. Men who won't get a manicure, pedicure, looking like a *linebacker*. Don't have nothing in his house—only thing he got is bottled water and *dick*. He ain't got *shit* else. How you ain't got no toilet paper and how you gonna wipe your ass? Got a dirty rag in there that smells like mildew. They ain't got *shit*. Yet, this man is gay as fuck! I see it *all* the time.

So, these expressions of what a man *should* or *shouldn't* be, or what a woman *should* or *shouldn't* be, put us in these *boxes*, and then we wonder why we keep having *fucked-up* relationships or no relationships at all. Because when we don't operate in our authentic self, we become a *repellent* to good things. For many of us, one of those good things is the type of person we're *actually* attracted to, not just the one we *think* we are (or think we should be) attracted to. I've said in previous chapters how in my twenties every man I dated was the hypermasculine type—the type I *thought* I wanted, thought I was attracted to. I thought I *liked* a man who wanted to lead and direct *all* the time.

Baby, I didn't.

I didn't like that he wanted to lead and direct *all* the time, and I didn't understand that hypermasculinity is often a *response* to insecurity. Because if you can't embrace any of your femininity *ever*, then you can't ever let your guard down, and you can't let nobody lead you, even when you're wrong, even when you *don't* know what you're doing. So, it *shouldn't* have been a surprise to me that these were the same men who *literally* had no ability to communicate during tough times. It shouldn't have been a surprise to me that these were the same men for whom, because they had such limited ability to communicate, it wasn't uncommon to put their *hands* on me when they got frustrated just because I spoke up. He didn't want to deal with me no more because he, and this is the exact quote, felt "*emasculated* in my presence." He didn't like it when I do XYZ. But, baby, *I* don't like it when you fuck up shit and *I* gotta suffer for it. The *fuck* I'm supposed to do? Sit and suffer because of your dumbass choices?

Nope, not me.

But I did for a *long* time before I learned this. And like I explained earlier, this attraction to him came out of the fact that our attractions are often guided by unresolved *trauma.* If you were a victim, you *will* seek out abusive partners until you're able to stop, reflect, and ask yourself, *Why is this my type?*

That question will come when you *properly* assess who you are and where you sit within your masculine and feminine energies. *My* choices in partners back then were governed by the fact that I didn't feel worthy or good enough myself. I felt *shy*; I was the *supporter*, the person always *waiting* in the background for my man to come in and save me, to protect me. That's why I zeroed in on those hypermasculine men who wouldn't let me have no time of day, and *that's* why I suffered with and put up with them for so long. But once I let *go* of this idea that femininity was the only way to be and *embraced* the fact that it's okay to have some masculine traits come out, I became more of a *magnet* for men who were more masculine *skewed* but who *actually* were vocal about saying, "I actually like the fact that you like to step up and lead." They *love* that shit. Oh, they *love* it. The men who are in tune with themselves love to let their partner lead where they are weak, and *they* love to lead where they are strong—see that? Balance.

And you know what the key is?

To *be* masculine when you *need* to be masculine, but don't *emasculate* him—just like you wouldn't want him to make you feel inferior when you're in your feminine energy. It goes both ways. What that means is if I need to step up and lead in a certain moment, then I'm doing it in a way that doesn't make it feel like I'm stepping up because *he's insufficient.* Or because *he's* not *doing* it good enough. I'm not doing it because *he's less than*; I'm doing it because I can see that this is something that I could do better for us, and it would benefit the both of us—and our partnership—for me to do it instead.

To put it verbally, it's like saying, "Do you mind if I take this? You did great but let me just try." You know, still laying on a bit of that femininity, but underneath it is that masculine energy moving things *forward.*

It's like rubbing his back while pushing him at the same time. I'm using my nurturing, sweet nature to rub his back, but that hand is also pushing with every rub. That's balance. It's not walking in front of him, grabbing him, dragging him, and saying, "Come on!" Don't yank his arm. That would be all masculine energy. And it's not sitting back letting him do everything, *knowing* he ain't going nowhere because he's not doing it right, but shutting up because you don't want to seem like you're taking over. That would be all feminine energy. You need both.

Rub his back *and* push him.

When it comes to balancing your masculine and feminine energies, look around and see that people out there, especially those in the younger generations, are doing just that. And I say that with certainty as someone raising two nephew-sons in their young adult years.

The other day, Marco saw Uzi, one of the rappers, wearing a Goyard crossbody bag, and in my day, we called those things a *purse*. It wouldn't be called no damn bag. But they call it a cross bag these days.

So he comes in one day with one, and he goes, "Whatchu think about this bag?"

I had to *catch* my damn self. In fact, I didn't even catch it right away. I went, "That purse?"

And he says, "It's a *cross bag*."

Well, excuse *me*. I'm sorry I ain't got the lingo right; it's all confusing these days anyway. But again, I did not catch myself. "Straight men wearing purses now?"

To his credit, Marco was completely unfazed. He just goes, "Yeah, Uzi is wearing it. It is what it is."

"Okay, if women don't mind seeing that."

His exact words were "I don't give a fuck what women want to see. I'm wearing what I *want* to wear. A woman gonna like me regardless."

Damn, son! Now, *that* is what I wanna hear, and I said, go on and *get* it. Do what you want to do! He wasn't asking for my permission, but my point is that his response was the *byproduct* of my teachings. And even though I was communicating some of my *own* bias to him, the fact of the matter was he was *confident* enough to say, I'm gonna be who I'm gonna be. A woman is gonna like me. She might be attracted to my confidence. I want a woman who is attracted to me for expressing myself. I don't want a woman where I gotta be who she *wants* me to be.

It is a *refreshing, much-needed* attitude among the younger generations. Because we live in a place where people go, *Ooh, there's something wrong with these men.* We *have* a new generation that's *comfortable* with releasing themselves from the gender *identities* that were *assigned* to them and are embracing their own unique *identities* and *expressions*. And they are *understanding* that how you express yourself in the world and who you go to bed with at night have *nothing* to do with one another. They're *done* trying to fit into the prescribed molds of older generations, and to all y'all older folk out there, there is some real value in doing that. But you can't get there without first examining who *you* are and being *okay* with accepting masculine and feminine energies in different spaces in your life.

Your journey is to accept that you are both and to find a complementary partner who's comfortable with how and where they operate in both.

Take Action to Get the F*ck Out Your Own Way

Do you lean more into your feminine or masculine energy? Can you identify areas of your life where your less-dominant energy might serve you better? And once you've done that, once you've accepted where YOU stand within your energies, take a look at the people with whom you have relationships or friendships. Where do THEY stand? Are they complementary to your own?

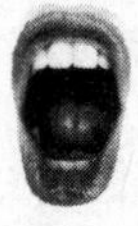

10

Top Drawer Yourself

If you want somebody to pay Mercedes prices for you, then you can't carry yourself around like a Corolla."

Who said TikTok can't be helpful? You can find some real gems out there, and believe it or not, that's where I heard this quote. It got me thinking about one of *my* favorite sayings: *Top drawer yourself.* This guy and I are saying the same thing: We've got to *package* ourselves better, in terms of personality *and* perspective, in order to attract whatever it is we want to attract—men, women, opportunity, *whatever* it may be. When I saw that, I wanted to throw my hands up and bless this goddamn beautiful stranger. *Preach* it, honey! I've been saying the same thing for *years*, just with a different term. Sometimes people *have* to hear something a different way for it to really sink *in*, you know?

To top drawer yourself is to be the *healthiest* version of yourself while knowing how to package your personality, aesthetics, mindset, and how you *present* yourself to the world in order to become a *magnet* for the kind of life you want to live. What this looks like will vary from person to person, but what we all have to recognize is that the life we want—the money, the job, the spouse, and the good relationship—comes by first assessing how we *already* present ourselves. That means asking questions like *What comes out of my mouth? How do I communicate? How do I dress? When I walk out the door, am I physically packaging myself in a way that's going to attract what I want to be attracted to me?*

These are questions I ask myself because I *physically* want to present myself in a way that makes me the healthiest version of me in that moment. It might look different for you, so you gotta figure out what your healthiest version is. But I'll let you in on a little secret: The *key* to a healthy you is *confidence.*

When I'm *dressed* nicely, I'm *smelling* nice, and my *hair* is together, I'm presenting myself in the best way—and that overall *aura* that I give off as a package becomes a *magnet* for people to want to *interact* with. That confidence I get from knowing I'm taking care of my body in the best way possible makes *me* more comfortable approaching people and going out there to look for what I want. I *know* that I get a *very* different reaction from people when I am *operating* in a space where I feel confident. People lean in more, they listen more intently, and they're more willing to strike up a conversation with me.

To top drawer yourself is to be your healthiest self by creating your most *confident* self. To package yourself *not* so that other people will like looking at you, but so that *you* can feel your most confident. Packaging in this way attracts things you want *to you*, but more important than anything else, it also has a *direct* connection with the level of confidence that *you* feel toward *yourself*. It is your *confidence*—not your *clothes*, your *weight*, or your *face*—that is the game-changer. But you're not gonna feel confident if you have not *first* packaged yourself in a way that makes *you* feel good about *you*.

We've talked about self-worth and how low self-worth leads to seeking out relationships that don't serve us, where we have to *chase* and act as *people pleasers*. It's the same with confidence. If you ain't *confident* in your*self*—in your ability to engage with the world and overcome problems—you are going to subconsciously *manifest* and seek out and *create* situations that *produce* what you *expect*. So, if I *think* that this whole world is fucked-up, and all these bitches are going to *try* me, and all these folks ain't worth *shit*, and blah, blah, blah, then what am I going to do? I'm going to seek out opportunities for where that's true, and when I *don't* find those opportunities, then I'm going to *create* them. Because, *ultimately*, our minds want to create outcomes that *validate* our expectations, *regardless* of how awful those expectations are.

If you are *under-confident*, you are going to let *fear* dictate your life. Take it from someone who used to do that shit *all* the goddamn time. There were a lot of opportunities I missed out on—dating opportunities, professional opportunities, just across the board—because I showed up in spaces *expecting* people to hurt me, take advantage of me, or treat me poorly. It wasn't uncommon for people to say I had an *attitude* problem because I would show up *anticipating* they would treat me or see me in a certain way—so I'd come prepared with my attitude in place, ready to defend myself. If I showed up like this, I was packaged for *confrontation*. If I showed up like that, I was packaged to be taken *advantage* of. If I showed up packaged as a Corolla instead of a Mercedes, you *bet* people would treat me like a damn Corolla. Most of the time I was packaged to not be *trusted* because I didn't trust nobody to begin with.

I used to always feel *defeated* before I even went into a room full of people. I didn't think anyone would like me, so what did I do? I went into rooms physically, but not mentally. I was *hyper-introverted*. I'd stand along the wall and just cower like I was shrinking into my skin. I told myself, *I'm just introverted and quiet.*

I *am* quiet at times, but this ain't one of them!

The truth is I was *afraid*. I was *fearful* that I was not going to be *accepted*. I didn't show anyone who I was. I thought I was *protecting* myself, but the reality was I was only creating my own self-fulfilling prophecy. Staying hidden and quiet meant that opportunities weren't coming to me. But then I'd say, "I knew I wasn't going to get that opportunity," not realizing that I'd shot myself in my own damn foot all along, and it didn't have to be that way. In many ways, I was doing it to *myself.* This goes back to what we talked about regarding owning our energies and how we package ourselves. Packaging ourselves well leads to confidence, which leads to us feeling comfortable and confident presenting our *true* selves to people *all* the time.

That fear of being ourselves shit comes from when you *haven't* top drawered yourself. So how do we fix that?

The *only* way we can work on our confidence is to understand *why* we are packaging ourselves in damaging ways in the first place. We've got to work *through* the things that are making us hurt ourselves, and we've got to be *honest* with ourselves about *how* we want to show up, so that we can be *intentional* about changing it and showing up that way. When friend after friend kept telling me the same story—*I really didn't even like you when I first met you*—you better *believe* it made me look at myself. That's what we need—honesty. From others *and* from ourselves.

I was, initially, being received as a stuck-up jerk at worst and a victim at best.

Then: How do you *want* to be received?

I wanted to be received as someone worth having around.

That's where my misalignment was. Those two things, my *want* and my *reality*, were on opposite ends of the world. Here's what it came down to: the stories that we tell ourselves *about* ourselves.

Those stories are the most *powerful* things that we have in our lives.

They are the magnets that *dictate* what direction we go in life. It's the stories we tell ourselves about ourselves that are the *foundation* of what kinds of relationships we'll have. And not just relationships, but *opportunities.* If you are *telling* yourself a story about yourself that is *negative*, that is *defeatist*, that has you as the *victim*, you are going to attract situations that will *keep* you in that negative state of mind, keep you *defeated* and, more importantly, keep you as a *victim.*

I went through a lot of shit in my life—sexual abuse being one of them—and from early on that stuck with me. *I'm a victim.* That was the story I kept telling myself about myself over and over again. It *became* me. In hindsight, it shouldn't have been a *surprise* that some of the relationships I kept having were with abusive men. I *sought* them out. Lack of confidence leads us to subconsciously look for situations that put us in an awful place. I *lived* it for so many years. I looked for these men because I believed that *I'm a victim. Everyone hurts me.* I *never* chose the right people. And when I found the *right* people, I wasn't attracted to them! Like, why can't I be attracted to the nice guys? The good guys? What's wrong with me?

It was because of the story I kept feeding myself. It was the *I'm a victim* mentality running through my head like a track on a goddamn loop, and I realized that I wasn't attracted to those nice guys because they weren't the kind of men that allowed me to *live out* the story I'd been telling myself about myself. I can't be no victim when a guy treats me good. Even though I didn't *like* going through all that shit and drama with those abusive men, on a subconscious level I was *attracted* to it. I was attracted to *them* because they fit into the stories I was saying about myself. They fit into the *identity* that I was more comfortable with, more *familiar* with, the *victim* attitude.

If you wanna change your packaging, you *have* to change the story that you tell yourself *about* yourself. Like any story, we gotta dissect the *foundation* upon which it was built. If your story is something negative, something defeatist, then it's a safe bet your foundation is *fear* or *doubt.* But stories don't just take shape based on a single emotion. They have something *else* paving the way—and that other thing is your *inner critic.*

An inner critic is that voice in your head that is the foundation of *doubt.* It is the voice within your mind that makes you second-guess your decisions. It is the voice within your mind that tells you that you ain't *good* enough. It is the voice within your mind that sabotages the *good* things you're trying to do in your life. It *stops* you from doing the things you need to do. It tells you, *Who are you to want more?* It tells you you're gonna fail anyway if you try to want more.

Your inner critic is a tape that runs over and *over* in your head, reinforcing negative thinking about yourself, stopping you from living your best life. It *stops* you from being able to make the amount of money that you truly are capable of making. It *stops* you from having fulfilling, healthy relationships. You can meet the *best* people on earth, but you're not going to be able to receive love *fully* from people when your inner critic is in your head telling you that you don't deserve it. Telling you you're not *good* enough, that you don't deserve love and friendship as good as that. You can only receive love at the level that you love yourself, and your inner critic *stops* you from loving yourself fully.

First, we gotta understand *where* this inner critic comes from. You might be thinking, *It's in my head, so it must come from me, right?* Wrong! The first step to taking the power from your inner critic is to recognize that the voice *isn't yours*. I ain't saying you're hearing other people's voices—you're not crazy—but what I am saying is that voice was not *created* by you.

Most people who struggle with an inner critic do not realize that their inner critic voice was created by some *other* area within their life. Perhaps it was a parent who constantly criticized you or made you feel like you were never good enough. Maybe you were picked on and called names as a kid. Maybe it was a past partner or spouse who was abusive. Maybe you developed an inner critic of yourself as a way to push yourself harder, faster, longer, and you never learned to turn that inner critic off.

I see this all the time: when folks are trying to make it out of a bad place, say, poverty, and they constantly push themselves to be better than everyone else—to never fuck up or make a mistake—so they can get to that better life that they've envisioned. But then, once they've used that inner critic voice to help drive them to where they wanted to be, then they are too in the habit of hearing it to turn it off again. Like that sour milk we talked about before, they kept that voice around too long and never threw it out once it was no longer good for them.

The reality is that our inner critics are often created by the relationships and experiences we have in our lives, and the *feedback* we keep hearing from them over and over again. Where *else* would this voice have come from? We're born with a clean *slate.* A baby don't come out of the womb with an inner critic or self-doubt. It's got to be acquired *someplace.* We often *learn* how to treat ourselves based on how others treat us during those formative years when we're the most impressionable. Think about that.

I was sitting talking to a friend one day and he was saying, "You know, Malcolm, I've been beating myself up constantly. Every time I try to make a good decision to advance my life, or make a good decision for my relationship, I hear that voice in my head."

I said, "What is that voice saying to you?"

"When it comes to my business, I say to myself, 'Why are you gonna take that step? Why you gonna take that risk? You know you're not able to do that. You're not good enough. You're not smart enough.'"

I said to him, "What about relationships? When you're trying to make a better choice for you and your wife, what do you hear then?"

"It's like, 'You're a good enough husband. You bring in money, but she just wants *too* much,' or, 'You can try to give her what she says she wants, but you're gonna fail anyway. Come on, you are who you are.'"

I said, "Wow, that's a really powerful voice. How often does it come up?"

"It comes up regularly."

I saw where he was coming from because God knows I know what it's like to deal with an inner critic. So I went, "Think back to early in your life. Who was the most critical voice in your life when you were a child?"

He thought back, thought back, thought back, and then he said, "My father. My father was the most critical voice in my life."

Now we were getting to the meat of things. So I asked him, "What kinds of things would he tell you?"

"Whenever I'd tell him I was gonna do something new and great in my life, he'd tell me, 'No, don't do that, you're gonna fail anyway.' When I was leaving for college and I wanted to go to another state, he said, 'Don't go there. You're not smart enough to be on your own in another state. Stay close to home so we can take care of you.'"

Bingo. I said, "Is it possible that your inner critic is actually the voice of your father that you've taken on within your own head, and now you play that voice out repeatedly within your life?"

He thought about it for a while before he said, "Damn, I never thought about it like that."

Think about what voice you heard early on in your life—a parent, a sibling, a friend—who was very prominent and sounds the most like the inner critic you hear now.

What did you hear?

Whom did you hear?

Once we know that, we can realize that our inner critics are not *us*. They are not our own voices. They are simply thought patterns that we have habitually *allowed* to continue, but they did not *start* with us.

Now that we know where our inner critic comes from, we can see how it leads to the stories we tell ourselves *about* ourselves. Our inner critic creates stories *for us* when we do not *allow* ourselves to sit in our feelings and push through them. We *define* ourselves by the stories we create surrounding those feelings.

For example, if you're hyper-introverted and you go out and meet someone new, that's a difficult situation already. But maybe you take a stab at it, and you invite them to hang out on Tuesday for a drink or to watch something. You want to make a new friend.

They decline, very politely, and say, "I'm not interested in that," or, "I already have plans that day." When they decline, your inner critic flares up.

Oh, I'm not good enough for them.

They rejected me. There must be something wrong with me.

What is it about me that made them decline my offer?

And what we *all* do that gives our inner critic power is create stories to go *along* with our feelings.

I feel hurt *because* I'm being rejected.

And I'm being rejected right now because I'm not good enough.

And I'm not good enough because I didn't do this or that.

And I didn't do this *because* I'm stupid, I'm bad at this, or I'm not *able* to do that.

You see how it just *continues* and snowballs? That's what happens when we create our own stories based on what our own inner critic has to say about us. We *justify* our feelings of unworthiness to ourselves, blaming ourselves even when we've done nothing wrong. In our most vulnerable moments, our inner critic will come up *strong*. It doesn't need your help! But you are *giving* it more power when you create that story about why you're sad, hurt, angry, or scared. When it gets that power, your inner critic will start putting *thoughts* in your head that will directly support whatever insecurities you already have. It will create a platform for your insecurities to become even more prominent, and that platform will become center stage in a way that *stops* you from being able to top drawer yourself. It *stops* you from living your best life, the life you *want*, all because of your inner critic.

So, baby, let's take a step back. Big breath, and let's work it out. Here's what I want you to do: The next time you find yourself in one of these moments, I want you to focus on what you *feel* rather than think about the *story* of what that feeling means. The next time something happens that makes your inner critic climb back up, step back and ask yourself, *What do I feel?*

Then, whatever it is you feel, put a *period* on it.

I feel *sad*.

I feel *hurt.*

I feel *rejected.*

I feel this, that, and that's *it.* There's no more to that sentence, honey; you just gotta leave it. You gotta *feel* it. The minute you start to go into stories and narratives that make it about *why did this happen* and *what could I have done to prevent this,* you're giving your inner critic room to expand within your mind to make the matter worse. You start spiraling into a narrative where you're beating yourself up, and you're creating a story that's not even based on what actually happened! Take our example from before. All you know is that that person said *no.* You don't know if they think you're good enough or not, so why create a story to tell yourself that? All you know is that they said no, so leave it at that. *My feelings are hurt.*

Allow yourself to sit with those feelings. They are *allowed* to exist within you. Once you can sit with just your feelings alone, I want y'all to ask yourself another question.

What is my truth?

Because, honey, your inner critic is *not* your truth. When we *allow* those stories in, they dominate our minds and we *let* them become our truth, and we have *such* a difficult time unlearning that shit. In that moment of whatever you're feeling—say you're feeling insufficient because he, she, or they did this and made you feel that way—*recognize* that feeling. *I feel insufficient.* But also realize that it's not a reflection that you actually *are* insufficient. It's just a thought pattern that's been there for a long, *long* time, and while it doesn't make you feel great, realize it is *not about you.*

It's just a habitual way of thinking that you are taking steps to break.

Remember that your inner critic is not facts. *Feelings* ain't even facts. Our feelings are valid reactions to what happens to and around us. The more y'all recognize that, the more *power* you will have over those feelings.

So, this is how I'm feeling. Maybe it's insufficiency. But what is the *truth* of the matter?

No, the truth is that I *am* sufficient. I *am* good enough. I *deserve* to be loved.

You may not always be able to speak your truth if you're struggling, and that's *okay*. You know what you do then? You call up a trusted family member or a friend and you ask *them*. Be honest with them; tell them what's up with you. "I'm struggling right now. My inner critic is telling me things about myself I know aren't true. Can you remind me of one or two things about myself that can help me come to terms with my power and bring me back to the present?"

Do *not* try to erase what you feel or erase what your inner critic is saying. That *never* works. In fact, it only makes it stronger because your inner critic feeds on your *fear*. But if you can learn to separate what you *feel* from what you know is your *truth*, then you can seek to understand your inner critic and take away its power to influence you. In doing so, you can *rewrite* the story you tell yourself *about* yourself.

Let's remind ourselves of the steps to top drawering yourself.

The first step is to recognize the problem. Recognize whether your wants and your reality are different. If that's the case, then you need to *package* yourself and show *up* in places differently, which ties into the stories we tell ourselves about ourselves and our attitudes toward ourselves and the world. I'm telling you this because so many of y'all have had an attitude for so much of your lives. We've been through so much that there's only one way we know how to operate. We don't know how to be easygoing! So what we do is we go with the familiar. Maybe you think life has worked out for you just fine. People don't fuck with me when I'm this way, and that's good. People may not be trying to fuck you over, but people also don't *fuck with* you. Opportunities aren't coming your *way*. People tell you what you want to hear just to *appease* you rather than tell you the truth, so your relationships are *fragile* and *inauthentic*.

When it comes *down* to it, we have to check in with ourselves and be honest about the stories we're telling ourselves about ourselves. Are they serving you? Are they undercutting your confidence? Are they making it difficult to top drawer yourself to get *after* the things you really *want* in your life?

That story you're so familiar with, that you *love* and hold on to, might just be the thing holding you *back* from the life you deserve. Don't let it do that no more. Identify your inner critic, be honest, and set your story straight, so you can package yourself for the life you want, showing that side of you to the world that will invite new people and opportunities *in*.

Take Action to Get the F*ck Out Your Own Way

How do you show up in this world, and how are you received? Does it align with how you WANT to be received? If not, ask yourself what stories you are telling yourself ABOUT yourself. Who are you in those stories–a victim, a people pleaser? If that person is not serving you and giving you the confidence to top drawer yourself, you gotta rewrite your story.

Identify your inner critic's voice. Whose is it, and where did it come from?

The next time your critic flares up, step back. Ask yourself what you feel and put a PERIOD on it.

Identify your truth. If you feel a certain emotion, that doesn't mean you ARE that. Remind yourself or ask someone else to remind you of who you are and what you can do.

Then, rewrite your story to be the person you WANT to be, so you can top drawer yourself and go after the life you deserve.

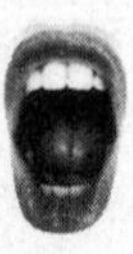

11

Find Your Core Competency

The stories we tell ourselves about ourselves don't just influence the types of situations we create and put ourselves in. They also affect our ability to know what we're good at. If you're painting yourself to be a constant victim and beating yourself up, then you ain't *ever* going to meet the goal of what *I* like to call our "core competency" and "unique-ability." You ain't *ever* gonna find true success in your life because those lies you keep telling yourself are gonna *keep* you from walking down your *true* path.

Your core competency is a skill set; it's the one thing that you've *always* done well. Maybe you know yours, maybe you don't, but that's what this chapter is gonna help you with. Unique-ability is being your authentic self. It's not just *one* skill set. It is literally when you are operating in the space of being who you authentically *are.* It's an *amalgamation* of *all* of your best traits coming together. Even in the areas where you're *not* strong, those things shine so bright that your less strong areas don't even *matter.*

You can't ever operate from an authentic place if you're *not* willing to be fully *honest* with yourself about who you are. Our most authentic selves can *only* come out when we are operating from a place of *confidence* and *self-assuredness.* But you can't be confident about who you are if you're not willing to *see* what makes you feel most confident. If you are not fully honest with yourself about who you are *across* the spectrum, then you're not going to allow your unique-abilities and your core competency to come out. That higher version of yourself will be *trapped,* and *you* will suffer for it.

The previous chapters helped y'all start on the journey of accepting and *knowing* who you are, but I know you'll come straight back here with the real question: How can I monetize who I *really* am?

It's a fair question, honey, and I'm gonna give you an equally fair answer.

Take money *off* the table.

I ain't *saying* money doesn't matter. Baby, you *know* I would *never* say that. I'm the *last* person on earth that would say, "Money doesn't *matter.* You don't need it to have a happy life." Fuck that and fuck anyone for saying that. Money is *great.* Have lots of it, please. What I *am* saying is take it off the table for *now,* while you figure out your core competency and unique-ability. Because you do *not* need to be in constant ka-*ching* mode when trying to figure out your path. But what I *always* stress is this: You may *not* be able to monetize every *aspect* of your unique-abilities, but you *can* find a way to monetize some of them.

The reality is that for *some* people being who they are in and of themselves *is* capable of being monetized into a full brand. For *others*, the fulfillment and rewards of operating in our unique selves might be that you're gonna have *healthy* relationships. Maybe you're going to have a great relationship with *yourself*—and *that* will lead to you having a healthier relationship with money. Being your authentic self and operating within your unique-abilities can reap rewards that are not always *just monetary*.

Once you've identified who you *truly* are—understanding your masculine and feminine energies—*own* the story that you tell yourself about yourself. Be *honest* with yourself about what you really like and what you really don't like—*that* will position you for opportunities that actually are in *alignment* with who you are. It will help you find your path to monetizing your core competencies and your unique-abilities. And *I* believe that when we find jobs and self-sustained work that are actually in *alignment* with who we are, that opens the door for us to be far more *successful* at them. Which ultimately *will*, for most people, mean making more money.

If you like to lead and direct, don't push that down and say, "Oh, that's too masculine—or too bold. I shouldn't lead and direct. I'm fine here in this role where I have no say-so." *Embrace* it. Get *rid* of your shame about that. Find yourself a job where you can tell people what to do because you are *good* at it. *That* is your core competency.

Now, I know what y'all are thinking. This seems like so much *work*! It feels *roundabout.* Well, honey, it's only roundabout because we all *went* the wrong direction in the first damn place! Had we *known* early on that the key to making successes of ourselves was to *embrace* who we authentically are, we would have been on the direct path the whole time. But it is what it is, and we're gonna make the *best* of where we are. I did, even after I took the wrong path after college, and look where I am now. I tell you, the path wasn't easy, but it was doable, and that's what matters. I have always been somebody who loves to lead and direct. I *love* to run the show when it comes to business. And what's the *perfect* job for someone who loves to be in charge? *Entrepreneur.* I have *wanted* to be an entrepreneur since I was *six.*

I didn't come from much in my household. We had enough to get by, but we weren't living no dream. While there were members of my family who were extremely wealthy, I never had *no* financial help from that side of the family—ain't *ever* seen a penny of their money—so I grew up with the poverty mindset for such a long time. When it came to actually running my own business, it was so hard to *change* how I viewed things. But I didn't pursue entrepreneurship for so long because it didn't fit within my idea of who I thought I was. And *that* is what I'm trying to warn y'all about.

Sure, I *loved* being in charge, I loved leading and directing, but at the same time, I was *ashamed* of my love for it. I didn't feel like it fit me. I didn't *feel* like that with all these women and all these feminine, gay men around me. They were so *feminine* and *comfortable* being feminine, I thought, *I need to do something feminine because I'm pretty just like them.* I didn't embrace my natural ability to lead and direct. I squashed it down underneath my shame and embarrassment and pretended I *liked* living and working the way I was. I did that for *years*, even after I graduated college.

My first years out of college I was in a strange *limbo* between my fake self and my true self. I *wanted* to be an entrepreneur, but—"ooh, *no*, I'm too *feminine* for that"—and I *didn't* want to be in corporate America because that was just all too *dry* and *boring*. Nothing seemed attractive about it. My friends were all going into their corporate jobs, and I was like, "Y'all telling me you are *excited* to sit in cubicles all day? Y'all *excited* just to get four weeks of vacation every year, to have a *limit* on your income?" No shame to anybody in corporate America because you *need* that experience to shape the foundation to *become* an entrepreneur. I did not want a traditional job, but I didn't have the *courage* to go after what I really wanted, either. I tried *every* small business you can imagine. I became a *nightclub* promoter, I pitched real estate, and I did everything I *could* to piece together enough income to support myself.

Then two years later, the Great Recession came, and y'all know how *that* story went down and how it affected businesses across the country. But that put me in a *tight* spot. Everywhere I was working was going out of business, and I was looking at being *forced* to work in corporate America. Then an opportunity landed in my *lap*. I got a *great* noncorporate job opportunity that a close friend recommended me for, and it was going to open the *door* for me to become a union representative and *advocate* for union workers whenever an issue came up. And it was *aligned* with my true self.

But *because* I was so comfortable feeding myself lies about who I was, I was *scared* to take on this opportunity. I just thought, *Oh my God. I'm gonna have to be running the show, and I don't want to take it on because I'm scared of that level of responsibility. I'm scared of stepping out of who I think I already am.*

That was my thinking, to go *against* what I felt was naturally a fit for me based on the *identity* I had in my mind about myself that I had *created* based on past trauma.

My friends, bless them, kept telling me, "You can do it. You'd be really good."

But that was *powerless* against my own voice. I was like, "Oh, *no*. I don't want to do that. I'm an *introvert*." This was true in my head, which I then manifested to be true in my *life*. Self-fulfilling prophecy in the worst way.

So, I took a corporate job working in Excel, doing financial consulting all day at Deloitte & Touche, the big accounting and consultant firm. I'd just started making over $100,000 a year for the first time in my life. I was just barely scratching over six figures, but I was happy to have made it to the six-figure club nonetheless. But the job was *not* fulfilling for me *at all.* First of all, it was fucking corporate America, the *one* thing I knew I did *not* want to get into. Second, I didn't get to interact with *people.* I was staring at a screen all the damn time, bored out of my fucking mind. I was alone in a cubicle for eight to ten hours every day, working in Excel or PowerPoint. Not to mention, I still had to deal with Karens every day and their microaggressions. And I also had to deal with the idea that I could get laid off at any time. I *hated* it. I was burning out because it *wasn't* working for me. And even though I didn't *enjoy* the job, I thought that was all I was *supposed* to do based on how I saw myself. So, I stuck with it. I stuck with it for *way* longer than I should have just to be able to *fit* into the story of who I kept telling myself I was. But after the luster and allure of making six figures wore off, I was like, "I still don't like this shit."

But, you might say, *you were making money at that time with the consulting job.* I was, honey, but I'm also making money *now*, operating in my unique-abilities. And who's to say how much further I could have been if I actually operated in them earlier? That's my point. Had I not turned down job opportunities like the union one, who *knows* where I could be now?

I could write a whole *book* just on what I missed out on because I wasn't leaning *into* who I authentically was. The *sooner* you lean into your unique-abilities, the earlier doors will open up and lead you to the *many* professional and personal opportunities that are in *alignment* with your abilities. You will have the chance to go much *further* and make far *more* money doing those things than by trying to do things that fit the version of you that you think you should be.

It is a saying as old as *shit* to find what you're good at, but fuck if it ain't true. Ladies, gents, y'all listen up. It is *imperative* to figure out who you are and find what you're good at—that is the recipe for all success in life. Take it from someone who has always *wanted* to be an entrepreneur but didn't start until much later in life than he should have. Once you've figured out your core competency and unique-abilities, *then* you can figure out how to monetize that shit. But let's backtrack for a moment, and I'll tell you how I got the *fuck* out of my rut.

I had some bright spots in my day, but they were too few. I liked talking with my coworkers about the problems they were going through in their personal lives. The best time was every Sunday night when I'd go home and do my YouTube vlog, which, at the time, very few people watched. But I didn't care about that. It was an outlet to keep me sane, even though they weren't paying me any money yet. But before I knew it, I had had *enough* of my full-time job. Everyone around me was either looking forward to the weekends or looking forward to retirement. I was like, *Y'all can't be happy* now? Some of us won't even *make it* to retirement, but, working this way, we gotta *wait* to be happy? For me, that sounded like misery, and I knew I didn't want to live that way anymore. And I remember thinking to myself one day, *I'm in my* twenties. *I gotta work like this for the next forty* years *just to get to the finish line?* Oh *hell* nah. That was such a depressing thought for me.

What have I been saying is the first rule to getting better? *Recognize the problem.* If you've been feeling this kind of way, be it in a relationship or a job, then *realize* it. That thought that I'd be stuck at a fucking cubicle not talking to anybody for forty-plus years made me *understand* that I didn't want to live that way anymore.

Then think about the way you *want* to live.

Just like how we discussed previously about top drawering yourself, ask yourself what it is you really want. And *typically*, people want to do something that they're *good* at, something they enjoy *because* they're good at it.

I kept wondering, *What am I actually good at?*

If it helps, you can ask yourself in a different way. *What are the things that I get the most compliments about in my overall life? What have people always told me I'm good at?*

And if that doesn't work, don't work yourself up in your head! Get out there and *ask* people. I *asked* family and friends, "What do you all think I'm good at? What do you think I'd be good at in a profession?"

I realized that what I was good at was right under my nose. They all said the same thing. "Oh, honey, you can *talk*. You're a really *good* talker." When I started thinking about those compliments, they all echoed the same idea. I was always complimented on my communication. In school, they always said

I was one of two extremes: Either I didn't talk, or I talked too much. That said something about me that I didn't even realize—that when I have something to *say*, baby, I *say* it! Or maybe I *did* realize this about myself deep down, but it didn't fit into the story I'd been telling myself—who was I to be doing better, and why would I step out of my femininity when everyone around me was *living* in theirs—so I *ignored* it.

Well, look out, world, 'cause I wasn't ignoring shit anymore!

The *more* I thought about it, and the *more* I heard it from others, the more I started to *believe* it myself. I am really *good* at talking. And I started *basking* in this realization of myself!

So, then what?

Okay, so you've thought about what you really want and asked yourself how you want to live. Then you used those questions to find your core competency. Hallelujah! But now what? We move to the next question.

What are jobs that I can do that'll allow me to exercise this skill or competency?

I was asking myself what jobs there were that would allow me to *talk*. I didn't know what those were. First, I thought about becoming a teacher. I thought about it seriously, but then I was like, *Do I want to deal with other people's children all day?* No, I did *not*.

I thought about becoming multiple things, so many things I can't even remember what most of them were. But I encourage y'all to do the same—go online and look up careers for people who like to do what you like to do. It ain't got to be fancy, just Google that shit. For me, I put in that search box *people who like to talk careers.*

I must've scrolled through hundreds of career lists in that time, my fucking eyes were glazing *over*. But what happened was I started to see a trend. *Sales* kept popping up on every list, jumping out at me every time. And I was like, I *do* like talking, I *do* like influencing people. It reminded me of the union job I'd turned down, which was *literally* about influencing people to understand the union officers' issue or complaint. So it was an iterative process of me finding what I wanted to do. And *because* I'd had an experience from that Excel cubicle job, I was like, *Maybe I* can *try sales.* It's a matter of being *open* to the *options* that exist for any one of these skill sets and competencies—and *not* immediately turning your back on them because of that outdated story about yourself.

The other iterative part of this process, the one that really struck home for me, was the fact that my grandmother happened to already be in insurance. And she'd been talking for a *long* time about me getting my insurance license. She was like, "You can do a lot of talking with that. You can influence people. Maybe you'll earn just enough so you can do that YouTube thing you like doing so much."

Lord Almighty, Grandma was *right.* But not right away. If you are new to the workforce, just graduated from college or graduate school, and you are on the path to figuring out that *your* core competency and unique-ability *are* monetizable, then go for it. Take that path *directly*. *But*, if you're like me, someone who took the indirect route for whatever reason, and you *have* a steady, nine-to-five job, don't be thinking you're just gonna jump off the cliff and quit. Uh-uh, no, baby, don't do that. It wasn't until three years *after* I joined corporate America that I started my own business. Even after that, it was *another* two to three years to get it off the ground.

I was Side Hustle Sally. This ain't to discourage you from pursuing your competencies and unique-ability, but to set y'all up to be *realistic*. It's hard work, baby, I know. But it will be *worth it*. Like I said before, if you *pursue* what you are good at, it will *open* you up to new possibilities. But it ain't a quick fix. There won't be no one dropping a million dollars in your lap overnight.

It was the same for me. I couldn't just drop what I had—I was working at a top consulting firm at the time—so I kept my day job and worked insurance as a side hustle once I got my license. During that time, I took the *bold* move of going to LA, and this was before I even had an inkling of wanting to be on TV. I *literally* went because the weather was nicer, and I was gonna be out on the streets selling insurance door-to-door outside of work hours. My videos, even though I was still vlogging, weren't any means of income yet. I didn't see them that way. I just wanted to sell insurance in nice weather; that was my logic.

So once I got out there, I was still working my day job. I'd get there in the morning with my iPad and an extra modem because no way was I gonna get on *their* system to do *my* work. My routine was to check my work emails, make sure there wasn't no fires to be put out, and show that I was *there*. Then, whenever an insurance call would come in, I'd go to the conference room to take it. I ain't have no shame about it! I *did* what I needed to do. Plus, let's face it: *Most* people in corporate America, we know you ain't putting in those doggone eight hours a day. I figured out my daily workflow and scheduled my insurance calls *around* that to optimize my time. I worked like that for *years* while working on my competency, my unique-ability, which was *talking*.

Whenever I had the *chance*, I would sell. I had the idea then that since I already *had* videos, I would use them to drum up interest, so that people would see *me*, and I could target them with my ads. Then I would make my calls. "This is MJ Harris, the person from the video you watched—yeah, the gay guy, uh-huh. I'm calling about insurance, uh-huh." And on and on.

Literally every day.

What ended up happening was people would say to me, "Oh, your videos are so good! You should try to be on TV."

That was everyone's suggestion because, in LA, everyone thinks that being on TV is the fucking gold standard. That's *everyone's* goal. But it wasn't mine at the time. Eventually, the curiosity got to me. I started to entertain the idea, just like I did with sales, because people could see it was part of my unique-ability. The idea of doing it for money was still off the table because I didn't think there was no way in hell I could make a living just running my mouth on TV, but I did it anyway. I put myself out there, I took some meetings, and then something *beautiful* happened. That chance—y'all remember the ones I talked about, the ones I said would come when you lean *into* your core competency and unique-ability—it fucking *came.*

And it came *fast.*

With me making more *regular* content for YouTube, one of my videos got reposted. It was my "Don't Go Broke Trying to Impress People" video. Angela Yee, one of the most popular radio DJs and social media influencers in New York at the time, shared my video on her personal page and business platform, which got me even more *visibility*. In fact, it was something like over forty million views in a thirty-day period. I got a *slew* of people messaging me, visiting my page, sending me inquiries, all wanting to become my clients *or* join my team.

That was a *huge* part of me growing my business, on top of other things like collaboration and outsourcing. But it *came* from me leaning into my unique-ability—my *talking.* My *influencing* through my YouTube vlog to *reach* people who were struggling with some aspect of their lives. *That's* where that success came from, and I'm using it here and now to show you that you can *also* take whatever your unique-ability is and *use* it in a way that's gonna kick open doors and land you opportunities. But you gotta put that work in and take a real *hard* look at yourself first. I had to go through a real thorough process to figure out who I was in order to *capitalize* on the skill sets and competencies that *allowed* me to transform my life and, as a benefit, start raking in the money.

But it could only become that once I took the idea of money *off* the damn table and worked on myself *first*. Asking myself, what is something that I *naturally, effortlessly* do well? That I've *always* done well—*not* narrowing down the question too far by asking myself what I do well that specifically can make money.

And remember, it ain't just got to be one thing! It could be *multiple* things. More power to you if you've got many unique-abilities! For example, perhaps who you are at your most authentic is an *amazing* listener. Google "great careers for good listeners." They're out there. Or maybe your unique-ability is that you're very bossy. Google "careers for people who are bossy." Look at those specific things, those careers or businesses that people excel in who *also* share that skill or competency. Use any resource available to you—find out what *others* have done and mimic it! *There ain't nothing new under the sun, baby*. So, don't be afraid to try something that someone else has already done rather than try to reinvent the wheel.

If you do your research, you're going to see a *lot* of results. Then, based on those results, ask yourself whether any of them resonate with you. Read through your lists. Notice patterns. Notice what sticks out to you, what makes you pause or think, *Hmm, that's something I could do*. Are you *interested* in any of them? If not, maybe another search will open a different door for you to find something you're really interested in.

So, there you have it, baby. The *key* to success, however that's defined for *you*, is to be authentically you and let *that*—your true self—guide you down the path you were always meant to go down. Start with taking money off the table and think about the *ability* and the *skill set.* If you *can* monetize it, great—fly to the moon, honey. But don't let no inauthenticity keep pulling you back to the ground.

Take Action to Get the F*ck Out Your Own Way

If you want to be successful, figuring out your core competency and unique-ability is paramount.

First, take money OFF the table. Don't even think about it.

Second, ask yourself what you're naturally, effortlessly good at. It might be many things, or it might just be one.

Look up careers and paths for people with that specific competency–do any resonate with you?

And just keep in mind that whatever path you take, you might not always be able to monetize it. But it will open you up to chances and opportunities in which your full, authentic self can thrive and find success.

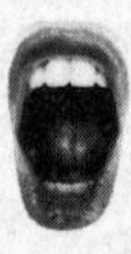

12

Life Ain't Fair, but You Can Still Get Your Money

Gather round, y'all, come in nice and close! We *know*, especially as people of color, that life ain't fair, but here's what I have to say to that: *Fuck* if life ain't fair!

As people of color, we can only level the hypothetical playing field so *far*. And it ain't just us—same if you're LGBTQ+, if you're *disabled*, if you're some form of *"other."* We all know what isn't said because we don't *have* to say it to know it, but I'm gonna say it anyway again and again, because the sooner we realize this, the sooner we can make decisions to get *around* it.

Life ain't *fair*.

It ain't *fair* that we gotta put up with other people's biases and attitudes just because we're viewed as "different" from the dominant group in some way. It ain't *fair* that we gotta work around those roadblocks just to get to the same place they are. And it's *easy* to get fucking mad and angry over these things. It's *okay* to be upset about a terrible double standard.

It's *great* to want to change things if you have the power to do so, but many of us don't. We *don't* have the power or the say individually to make these huge changes for all of humanity. But I'm *not* saying roll over and just deal with it.

What I *am* saying is it don't gotta be all *bad*. Stop *wallowing* in that self-pity and take some *agency* like we've been talking about. Get up, get started, and get *going*. It doesn't matter that life ain't fair because you can *still* get your money. When someone tells you, or you tell yourself, life ain't fair, remember these sweet five words coming right back:

Fuck if things ain't fair!

You heard me. *Fuck* fairness! *Fuck* what you gotta do to level the playing field!

Because life isn't *about* being fair, honey, it's about our *choices*. I've *never* had the idea that life is fair. *Shit*, if life was fair, I would not have had to deal with sexual abuse, being teased in school, the silent treatment throughout my upbringing, and abusive relationships as an adult. I learned *very* early that this shit is not *fair*. I *never* had the illusion that life was fair. I never felt *entitled* to feeling like life was fair because I just *knew* it: Ain't nothing fair *about* life.

But whether you realize that early on or much later, what we all *do* have a fair amount of is the free *will* to make choices that can *orchestrate* the kind of life we desire. *That's* what I focus on. I focus on the *choices* that I can make. I focus on the fact that it's not about what the *situation* is; it's about what I can *do* with the situation in order to create the outcome that I *want*.

Life is whatever we can make of it. So once we can begin to *own* that fact, it *is* up to us to *regain* that degree of control for ourselves over our lives and our mindsets. We feel far more *empowered*, which was something I struggled with growing up in a church-dominated environment in the South. Growing up, one thing that used to *always* bother me was when we'd be having a discussion and my parents would say, "Well, if it's the Lord's will..." and *leave* it at that, as if to say it's outta our hands. Leave it to *God*. Well, hang on, now! But don't you get free will, too? Don't the Bible say something about *your* free will? I ain't trying to deny the power of God, but I'm saying we have to realize that *we* have influence in this, too. We have some agency within whatever situation to be able to *choose* how we want to live. We don't have to be some *passive* bystander to whatever life throws at us. Who the hell wants to live life like that?

As I got older, I started to see that the people who made the *most* money or had the *most* success were those who *didn't* have a perfect life but who got *through* things quicker and easier. They were the ones who took *control* of their situations, who took *ownership* of the choices they had, versus people sitting passively on the sidelines waiting for others to *save* them. Waiting for others to *bring* them up. Baby, that wasn't me, and I *know* it ain't you. Be your *own* come-up.

There's a common saying in Black communities that we gotta work twice as hard to get half as far as white people. It *is* true, to an extent. We all have certain realities we gotta deal with. Some people are gonna have expectations of me that are actually *fair*, and some people are not. I ask myself, *What do I need to do that doesn't compromise my integrity and doesn't compromise my authenticity in order to achieve the financial success I want? What aspects of myself—because we're all multifaceted—do I need to bring to the forefront in order to get my money?*

I'm gonna embrace the reality of my situation and *use* that acceptance to do what I have to do to get what I need to *get* out of said reality. In *doing* so, I exercise far more *power* and *control* over my reality than their bias *ever* could. What I'm going to do is accept it *exactly* as it fucking is, and I'm gonna make the *choice* to get as much out of this as I can. Because I ain't *looking* for fair!

Lemme tell you a story. As a gay Black man, I never had *no* seats at nobody's goddamn table. When I moved to LA and decided to shoot my shot with the entertainment industry, I dealt with all *sorts* of inflated egos and high-and-mighty biases. After I put my name out there to be on this show or that one, I started to get some callbacks. I remember this one meeting where I was fucking *tap*-dancing—and I don't even know *how* to tap-dance.

I went into this room with these development executives and producers, the people who sit around and say, "I went to Northwestern, Yale, or Harvard." I ain't against education, but y'all know the kind of people I'm describing. *Culturally*, these people have no connection to you in any way, shape, or form. These people are *highly* educated, but they have *no* connection to the *human* component that makes *you* who you are and makes your *audience* buy into who you are. They, essentially, wanted to whitewash me.

Every *fucking* meeting, it was *Queer Eye* this, *Queer Eye* that! We could make you like, the *Queer Eye*, but the financial version. I wanted to say, "You do understand that just *because* I'm a gay man does not mean I can only do *one* format that five very talented gay men already did, right?"

As much as I fucking wanted to, I couldn't *say* exactly that at that point in time. Because I was sitting at *their* table, and when you're finding your ground, your footing, your *space*, at the end of the day, sometimes you *do* have to take a seat at somebody else's table. But you don't *stay* there. Because the only reason I'm sitting at your table is to learn *how* you run your table so I can go create my *own*. I ain't sitting dependent on your table forever, you hear? But in the meantime, while we're still learning, there ain't nothing wrong with being there *if* it serves you and helps you create your own table later on.

Trying to get a seat at other people's tables leaves you open for *them* to dictate the terms of how you can get and *maintain* that seat. It means you're never safe. That's why I say to never stay at another's table for long. Always have an exit plan. Always focus on not *keeping* your seat, but the tools to build your own table and the seats around it. Because whatever that means, however *long* it takes, however *slow* it goes, and even if it's not as *profitable* as what these folks can offer you, the one *great* thing is that *you* are in control, and ain't *nobody* who can take that away from you. If *you* build your table and your seat, only *you* can give them up.

Take Action to Get the F*ck Out Your Own Way

Life ain't fair, so stop looking for fair. Evaluate your choices. Life is what we make of it, so make it great! What are the realities of your situation? Whom do you have to deal with, and how do you have to package yourself to influence what you want out of the situation?

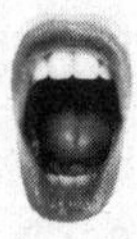

13

Don't Go Broke Trying to Impress People

Now we know how to get our money: Make *choices* and be *active*. Don't get sucked into dealing with other people's biases, and package yourself in a way to get what you want out of that person or that situation. But once you *have* some money, then what? We've discussed various forms of self-abuse and how to work through our shit so that we don't fall into that endless self-abuse cycle—or so we can get our asses *out* of that cycle. But there's a *big* one that somehow manages to fly under the radar, and that is *financial abuse.*

Money is a resource necessary for *survival.* We know that. But we often *also* see it as a source of our *power* and *confidence.* And it's *very* easy to conflate those ideas into *I should spend more to show how well I'm doing.* When you are using money in such an *unbalanced* way—spending, spending, spending with little to no saving as a way to *impress* people—that means you're *overspending.* By overspending, you are *compromising your own ability to survive* for the sake of momentary pleasure.

When you use money to try to impress people, you believe that you are so *insufficient*, you are so *unworthy* of positive attention on your own merit, that the *only* way to feel sufficient and to feel worthy is to *harm* yourself financially and compromise your *stability* just for the sake of other people's validation. You have *undervalued* your own *survival* because you *overvalue* what other people think about you. This is called *over-functioning financially.*

In the previous chapter we talked about how to get your money, but if you're in a self-abuse cycle right *now*, you gotta understand that even if you *get* your money, you're just gonna squander it to gain validation from others. But I'm here to show you differently—you ain't gotta pander to your feelings of insecurity and inferiority no more, not if you're aiming to get *better.* So, come on, get comfortable. It's time to understand what financial self-abuse looks like.

As with every other form of self-abuse we've covered, financial abuse is often a *manifestation* of unresolved pain. We have different labels for different abuses because they manifest themselves in different ways, which is common for *unprocessed* pain. Some people become workaholics. Others self-harm. But financial abuse, it manifests when you either lose control of your money because you're trying to impress other people, or you allow someone to control *you* through your money. Let's take a look at what both of these fucked-up instances look like.

When I first started to make really *good* money, I had the mindset that I had to do everything in a *way* that reflected the level of success I had accomplished. I was thinking, *I'm doing so much better*, so the *first* thing I did was spend more money. I bought a home, which is a great investment if it lines up with your financial goals, but the list didn't stop there. The next thing was, well, I needed to furnish this home, and it needed to *look* like a home that someone with my paycheck would *have*. I bought more expensive furniture. Then it was a new *car* because I *deserved* to have a better car—a car that warranted more money because I *had* that money now. And so on and so on.

I *told* myself that I *deserved* this and that, but what really was underneath that was *I needed to impress other people*. I was seeking *validation* from other people, but I was *hurting* myself at the same time because I wasn't *creating* wealth. I was making money but I was *spending* just as much, sometimes *more*, to gain other people's validation.

We've talked about over-functioning before, especially when it comes to relationships that don't serve us, and the same is true here: It all comes down to us occupying a bad mental and emotional space. Anytime we're over-functioning as a constant practice, we can't see our own *worth* and *value*. We financially over-function so that we can feel *loved* and *accepted* because we don't love and accept *ourselves.* We look to others to *give* us these feelings through validation, social acceptance, and praise because we are incapable of doing so for ourselves. In order to *achieve* those feelings through money, we *over-function*, we *overextend*, and we go *broke*. Everything *about* over-functioning comes from the need to *keep* certain people in our lives. We are *afraid* of them leaving, of them *viewing* us in a certain way, so we *overwork* and often drain our own financial resources in the process.

Uh-*uh*, not anymore.

I am here to tell you that this is the end of the *road* for such behavior. To get the ball rolling so that *we* control our money and do not let it control *us*, we first gotta understand our shame. Shame is the *root* of any over-functioning in our lives, and just like I've said throughout this book, we need to figure out the *source* of our shame because that shame is the thing we need to overcome in order to *stop* abusing ourselves. What was it in your past that cultivated this shame? Where did it stem from?

Our shame doesn't always come from one place, and in the financial game, one responsible party we *have* to look at is social media.

We all know the *majority* of social media users use their platforms to promote the *best* of themselves and their surroundings. We *know* what we see on social media ain't the whole truth—ain't nobody's life just a rolling snapshot of picture-perfect moments, like, come on. We know you ain't telling us the truth! Ain't nobody going out there and spending thousands upon *thousands* of their hard-earned money every *day* on luxury goods and month-long vacations to tropical islands and shit. We *know* so much of what we see is a fabrication, but *despite* that, despite knowing what we know, we *still* feel the pressure to do the same. Against all reasonable and *logical* thinking, somehow, we're *still* sucked into the "perfect life" ideal. And out of *that* pressure comes our shame that we *don't* post picture-perfect videos and reels all the time, shame that we don't *appear* to have the same lifestyle as what we see online, and shame about our current circumstances that, in all likelihood, are a mix of the bad, the good, the ugly, the beautiful, the problematic, the *real.*

And that's the issue.

We don't think anybody wants to *see* the real.

And we feel absurdly *ashamed* of *having* a real life. That don't make *no* sense!

Going broke to impress others ain't no new concept, but it has been exacerbated in the age of technology. It'll only get *worse.* Let me tell you something. I love, *love* being showy. I love to go in and give the *glamour.* I *love* it. I could *easily* be one of those people you see online, in every video, dressed to the nines and all done up and ooh, look at my nails, look at my *hair*, look at this, look at *that.* But what I have learned over the years is that it is not *sustainable* to show up like that online. It is not *sustainable*, it is not *healthy*, it is not *realistic.*

As business owners, we go through *ebbs* and *flows*. And it doesn't stop. I don't care if you're a billionaire, you will *still* go through financial ebbs and flows, it's just the nature of *any* business. I don't know too many business owners out there who can say it's *always* up and everything is *always* going. That's not *my* reality. So what I had to do was *accept* that and give myself permission that it's *okay*. It's *okay* to tell people, "I'm not doing that because I don't want to spend the money on that; that's not something that's good for me, financially, right now."

Ooh, that used to tear me *up*, but saying you can't afford to do something right now doesn't mean that you're *broke*; it doesn't mean you're not *good* enough; it doesn't mean you're *less* than somebody else. It means *the money that is required for this I have not allocated for that purpose. Therefore, I have to decline.* That's all!

It's okay to be *real* with people. Being real does not mean that you're not *smart*. All it means is that you're having a *human* experience, and that you're confident enough to be real about that human experience, rather than just being a blind follower, trying to keep up with the damn Joneses to impress *other* people. In human experiences, sometimes your money's funny, sometimes your money's not. It ebbs and it *flows*.

People *like* authenticity. They *like* it when you show them who you are up front, the *whole* you, not just some pretty, made-up-for-social-media you. And I'll tell you I felt much more *empowerment* through being *honest* with people not just about my ups but especially about my *downs* financially, because I no longer held on to that shame. When you let go of thinking that real life is *shameful*, you open yourself up to no longer having secrets—and those secrets just hold back your *empowerment.* You can't empower yourself if you're constantly keeping secrets because you always feel like you gotta *prove* something to someone else. Ain't shit empowering about that.

There's something to be said, too, about how these feelings of shame and unworthiness hit us early *on* as we're making money. I spent *more* to impress people during the times when I had the *least* money. You know why? Because in my mind, I needed to cover up my money situation that much *more.* I had some real, *deep-seated* shame about what was going on in my life, financially and otherwise. I was *ashamed* I didn't have *more* money to throw around, so I felt the need to cover it up by spending amounts I didn't *have.*

But not anymore.

Y'know the funniest thing is, I've got *way* more money now than I did back then, when I was spending X amount to *appear* like the person I thought others wanted me to be! But I don't mess with no shame cards anymore. Because when you don't have nothing to prove to anybody else, that's when you can finally get to *creating* wealth.

At the end of the day, making wealth is not about what you *earn.* It's about what you *spend.* It's the difference between those two amounts, in between the *gap*, as I call it. *That's* where your money grows, and the *only* way it's gonna grow is if you spend *less* than what you make—*consistently*. What's the *point* in living fabulous if you ain't got no financial safety to lean on in your older years or in your leaner months when money ain't flowing as consistently? We *need* some sort of savings, and if we're too busy spending to impress other people, well, then we're gonna be some very fabulous-looking broke people in a decade.

Once I sorted out my self-esteem issues, my *shame* issues, I knew that I would no longer use money as a way to seek validation from others. That was the moment I was able to start saving money and to start making *authentic*, *healthy* decisions for myself. Decisions that reflect who *I* am, even if they're not decisions that will impress—or even make sense to—other people.

Like my move to Bali. It was a *big* move that almost nobody in my family and friends understood. At that time, I was dealing with the risk of burning out. I was *exhausted*. I was *considering* what this burnout meant: Did it mean I needed to get *rest*, or did it mean I don't need to be *doing* some aspects of what I'm doing anymore? What if I'm *over-functioning*? And am I gonna *stop* over-functioning and cut some things back? And, if *so*, what would that mean for me financially? That was all the shit running through my head.

What didn't make sense to people was that I wanted to *reduce* some of my financial pressure when nothing bad was *happening* financially. The problem was things were going really *well*, and it *required* a lot of work to *make* those things go really well. Living in a multi-million-dollar house in the suburbs of Los Angeles, with the level of expenses and lifestyle that *comes* with that, was not something I *felt* like I could make choices about from a clear state of mind at that time. What my life was trying to authentically tell me to do for myself—take a step back, you're running yourself *ragged*—was not lining up with what I needed to do to keep up my lifestyle. I didn't feel like I could *do* that, take my foot off the gas pedal, so to speak, with that level of financial pressure on me.

My first thought was *My nephew-sons and I will just get a different home*. Marco and DJ had both come to live with me, making me a new parent to young adult boys who'd come under my care to find a new direction for their lives. I was now their guide into young adulthood, so I had to consider how moving to a different home would be a big change for them, too. But then I thought, *Just getting a new home here* might *work, but you'd still be in LA. You'd still be around people with an immense amount of pressure, in a* culture *where you constantly have to work, work, work*. The problem was mainly the cultural *value* around work where I lived. I started to think, *Where could I go where there's a different value around one's work?* I thought about different places in the United States, and I didn't wanna live in any of them.

Then, it just happened that I was going to Bali. I was supposed to go for just a two-week trip, and it got me thinking, *You know, this might work*. So I made a choice that I could make *because* I was not worried about how it was gonna be received or how people would *take* the news.

I talked to Marco and DJ, and I said, "What if we go out there and if we like it, we stay."

"Well, how long we gonna stay?"

"Until we feel like we don't want to anymore."

"What're we gonna do with the house?"

"We'll pack it up and put somebody else in it."

I told them the benefit for *all* of us was that we were gonna be able to be in an environment where we could spend far *less* money, which is, of course, very appealing no matter *what* your financial status is. But we were *also* going to be in a place where there's not *such* a big cultural value placed on the *work* mentality. So we would have more *free* time in our lives *and* in our days *mentally* to experience things differently. That would add *value* to our lives. I knew it would be better for them. 'Cause my thing is, what's better for me is gonna be better for them.

A lot of parents struggle with making decisions that are good for themselves; they always put the kids first, but I think it should be the opposite way around. You have to put *yourself* first, 'cause if you're healthy, whole, and financially strong—then you have something to guide them with. You have something more to offer them and nourish them with. You can't be your best self for your kids if you're depressed, anxious, can't sleep, and working like a hound. So, when I did consider them, I thought it'd be great for them to be able to experience different parts of the world. If they do choose to live in the States or anywhere else, at least they've had an option to choose from.

A lot of people say, "I chose to live in the United States." No, you didn't. You didn't *choose* the United States. This is where you're from and you never saw anything else. That's different than seeing the world and then having the option to *choose* where you want to be. I wanted that for Marco and DJ. I wanted them to at least know that they chose where they were in life. And how can they make an informed decision if they haven't seen anything else?

I'd found myself back in the same grind of constant work that I felt back before I'd left my consulting job. I was beginning to feel the same feeling of unhappiness and feeling stuck. I was starting to think, *I got more money and I got a better shoe closet, but there can still be more to life than this.*

I made a *choice* that a lot of people aren't willing to make, and I was very comfortable being *transparent* about that choice. I put up videos showing the whole *process*. I didn't leave nothing out. Because I'm not ashamed of saying that even though things are going well for me financially, I don't like what it takes to *maintain* this kind of life financially. Baby, I do not *care* if my decision does not make sense to *you* financially. Instead, I'm going to *put* myself in a position—even if it makes me look crazy—to do what I *feel* is right for me because impressing you all is *not* my priority.

Living happy and whole *is* my priority. Let it be yours, too.

***

Once I was able to take a step back from *over-functioning* in my life in order to maintain my finances, I was also able to open myself up to realizing that I had a history of both over-functioning *and* under-functioning at various times in my life, all rooted in that feeling of shame or low self-esteem.

Now, *under*-functioning financially, honey—*that's* one we need to talk about, too! Financially under-functioning is the opposite of *over-functioning*; it's where you ain't throwing all your money away to impress people, but instead always playing the *back seat* and giving up opportunities, accepting *less*, so that you can please someone else.

Low self-esteem is the ultimate player in our self-abuse, and it ain't no different when it comes to money. When it comes to *under*-functioning with your money, you think you ain't worth *nothing*, so your *money* ain't worth nothing, either. If you under-value *yourself*, then how is that gonna manifest in your opportunities to *make* money, then to hold *on* to that money?

I'll tell you, baby. It ain't gonna manifest in a way that serves *you*.

I'll tell y'all something: I once quit my *job* so that my man could take care of me. But I did this before he even showed and proved to me that he was someone who could *handle* being in that degree of power without using it as a form of abuse or control. I did it because of my sense of feeling *unworthy* at the time. Because I didn't feel good *enough*, I *under-functioned* so that he could *over-function*. I did less so that he could feel manly in his role of taking care of me, even though I knew damn well that I was capable of doing more and of taking care of business in my own right. Remember that conversation we had before about not being balanced in your masculine and feminine energies? Well, honey, *neither* of us were here, and *that* ended up being a travesty of a relationship! I was trying to be too much in my feminine energies, under-functioning because I devalued myself and was afraid that if I did more, it would scare him away, and he was trying to be too much in his masculine energies, over-functioning because it gave him a sense of power. See how our past traumas and shame *all* tie together in various areas of our lives?

Now, what have I always said about self-abuse? *Take some responsibility!* Honey, you *know* this problem stems from *you*—from whatever trauma you're still holding on to. And you *know* it takes two to tango when it comes to abuse involving two *adults* with the *agency* to leave if they wanted to. It takes *two* to tango.

For me to be in a dynamic where someone is *financially* abusing me—whether it's causing me to over-function or to under-function—means it was a *progressive* process where *I* gave up control over *time* to allow them to have that degree of financial control over me. For some people, it's giving up their job. For others, it's downgrading the lifestyle that makes them happy so that their man can feel manly in taking care of them. And for some of us, it's letting people use us—steal our money or spend it right from under us—just so that they'll stay around, accept us, and not abandon us.

So, honey, realize that financial abuse ain't no different than any other form of abuse we've talked about. When I have unresolved pain and unresolved trauma within myself that affects my own sense of self-esteem and self-identity in a negative way, it opens the door for me to allow *other* people to treat me as I treat myself. Because I am so *used* to mistreating myself—it's the only role I *know* how to play in the story I tell myself about myself—it's just easier to allow it and *stay* in such situations. You are *staying* there to allow this to happen. It's like putting your cheek out and saying, "Slap me. Slap me, slap me!" The very act of you staying there, with someone who financially or otherwise abuses you, is a *physical* manifestation of the abuse that you are doing to yourself internally.

If you find yourself having poor financial boundaries, there normally is some kind of unworked-through trauma that's up under there because money is simply a barometer or reflection of whatever else is working and not working within your relationship with yourself. To work through that trauma, you've got to go back to the beginning and *own your shit. That's* the first step to working through it, so you may need to read that chapter and the ones after it again—and that's alright! That's what we're here for, honey!

Take Action to Get the F*ck Out Your Own Way

There are three main steps to making your money and growing it. First, figure out if you're stuck in a self-abuse cycle–do you financially abuse yourself?

Do NOT try to impress people with your money or seek their validation USING your money. Stop that shit. Figure out the why behind your over-functioning: Are you ashamed of something? What is it? Then let it go. Understand that although we LOVE to show our perfect lives online, that ain't a reality for anyone. Baby, it don't matter if you can't afford such-and-such–own it! That will empower you to make choices that are healthy and authentic for YOU. It will allow you to save your money instead of spending it on things and people to make them stay.

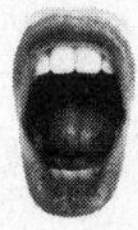

14

Survivor's Remorse—Be Unapologetic about Protecting Yourself and Your Money

Now that we know how to *get* our money and save it instead of going broke *impressing* people with it or letting others control us financially, let's flip a switch and talk about the other side of the financial spectrum: once you've *made* it.

With all the elation and the happiness surrounding you in a moment where you *should* be over the fucking moon and flying *high*, oftentimes we have a terrible little feeling that creeps up on us and refuses to go away. It's *guilt*. It's *anguish* over a come-up that was *solely* our own. Why, oh *why* are we feeling this way?

Take it from someone with a little too much expertise in the matter. What you're feeling is what I felt for a *long*-ass time.

It's survivor's remorse.

Survivor's remorse is feeling *guilty* for changing and growing—for getting *better*—when others around you, often those you know or love, have not. It's feeling guilty for getting out of a bad situation when others around you haven't or weren't able to. And it is *very* common in our generation and in our communities that we feel the need to try to pull everyone *else* out of it, too. That thinking and behavior keep us *tied* to relationships that no longer reflect who we *are*. And because we don't want to let people go, we hold *on* to our guilt at passing them up so that we can keep holding on to those old relationships. In the most extreme cases of survivor's remorse, people sacrifice *everything* that they have built, yet *they* are the only ones suffering from their financial over-functioning.

I'm gonna call it like I see it: Survivor's remorse is a very *costly* form of self-abuse. It makes us *over-function*, makes us *deal* with shit we *shouldn't* be dealing with, namely, what others want from us now that we *have* made it emotionally and financially. You try to save everybody, maybe trying to be the savior for your whole family, but then you end up sacrificing yourself or they end up bringing *you* down.

I'm not saying wanting to help people is *bad*. But it's when people *expect* your help, especially financially, and *expect* you to come bail them out at every chance. And when *you* expect that of yourself without them even having to call you up—this becomes a problem. It's a *classic* symptom of survivor's remorse. I'm an expert in this shit. I know exactly how it'll end.

I have a very helping spirit. I come from a family of people who help. My mother is a trained social worker who became a therapist and, eventually, a reverend. My father works in the community teaching people about their culture and helps them in so many different ways. I grew into an adult who believed that if you have the *means*, you should be helping everybody.

Everybody.

Help him, her, them, it, *whoever*. If you see potential in someone to live a better life or a different life, then you need to help them out.

Keep listening, honey, keep listening. This is for you, and it's about to get *real*. For you, for me, for everyone out there like us.

People like us, people who *love* to help, when we see potential in someone, we think, *I should be utilizing my gift to help change them. I should help* position *them so they can live a better life, a different life, like I've been able to do.* And then we *over-function*. We work to help this person be better and do better, and by the end we are burned *out*. We are *upset*, *mad*, and feel underappreciated by ourselves *and* others.

When I first started doing well, back in my late twenties, right after I started *tasting* a little fame and success, I was hit like a *truck* by survivor's remorse. My friends and family, it was like they came out of the freakin' *woodwork*—like they could *smell* the money on me. *Ooh, baby, you doing so well, you can share, can't you? Oh, honey, if only I had some of what you have, I could be doing this and that—if only I just had a little. Think you can help me out?*

And I gave in to all of them. I did. I gave people things they did not *deserve* because I did not know how to protect myself and my money. I wanted to *keep* them in my life, and I thought that by buying things, it would keep them in my life. And it did—but it also changed the way they *saw* me.

When you give someone something they don't deserve, they *undervalue* your gift. And because they undervalue the *gift*, that then leads to them undervaluing the gift *giver*. Giving people things they don't deserve or didn't earn ends up in a similar outcome as when Powerball lottery winners end up broke after just a few months. When people don't earn shit, they don't value it, and they squander it.

When I showed up at the next family or friends event with the thing they "always wanted but couldn't afford," they'd want it from me. You got it, so help me come up, too. They'd run to big ol' fancy new MJ, the cash *cow*, and they'd *ultimately* piss all over me *and* the gifts I was giving.

But you know what?

The truth of the matter was *I* was the one over-functioning trying to *be* their come-up because *I* felt guilty about them not living the life I had. They might have put pressure on me by saying all the things they'd done for me in the past, but *ultimately*, it was my choice. I *bought* those things. I *gave* them stuff they did not deserve, and I *asked* for them to treat me exactly the way they did because I was not valuing *myself.* So why would they treat me any better than I was treating myself just because I'd bought them some stuff? They wouldn't because they knew they didn't have to.

As with all other forms of self-abuse, survivor's remorse comes back to how *we* see and think of ourselves. It is connected to a lack of positivity about *yourself,* and in this case, it flirts with another heavy lifter of self-abuse: imposter syndrome. Y'all ever think to yourself, *Who do you think you are to be doing this?* Or if you're trying to stand your ground after your come-up, anyone ever come around you and say shit like "Oh, so you not gonna help me? I *know* who you *really* are!" An undercover threat, so to speak. That is people, yourself included, pushing imposter syndrome on you, making you *think,* making you *believe,* that you ain't worth all the good that's happened to you. Ring a bell?

Imposter syndrome and survivor's remorse go hand in hand. They are like the twin pillars of *evil.* They can drag you down, bury you underneath all this shit and toxicity so that you never come back up. They don't care about your protection. They only want you to continue projecting your negative self-image so that you can't enjoy the fruits of your labor as you should. But they can only do that if you *let* them.

When I became more known in LA, fame brought me both success and imposter syndrome. And even though I had *worked* for my success, even though I was my *own* come-up, I dealt with imposter syndrome for a very long time. I started to have people come up to me on the street and compliment me, saying things like "I *love* your work," or, "You changed my life." Person after person would come up saying variations of all this, and to every one of them, I'd say, "Thank you. Thank you so much. Would you like a picture?"

I was like fucking Mickey Mouse at an amusement park, snapping photo after photo after *photo* with every little kid running up to me saying I was their favorite. And you might think, *Well, what's so bad about that? You're getting people to like you; ain't that part of your job being on YouTube?* Sure it is, but the other part of it was that I couldn't *embrace* what they were saying because I didn't think I *deserved* it. So I'd just say thank you, snap the picture, and go. My behavior was my way of *deflecting* that praise because I didn't think I'd *earned* their praise. I thought I'd just gotten *lucky*. I didn't see myself as changing anyone's life.

Don't get me wrong, I enjoyed what I *did*. I knew it'd help people in some way, but I still felt like an imposter. I didn't feel like I had *earned* the right to be within the space I was in because I viewed *myself* in such a negative, low way. Even within my success I didn't feel *worthy*. Even with the *rewards* of operating within my unique-ability, I didn't feel *worthy* of them. I didn't *value* myself or my professional accolades and accomplishments. In some cases, it may be that we simply don't value what we bring to the table—we think, *I'm just starting out. I'm so inexperienced.* And even if we *do* value ourselves as people, we don't value our *work*. Both of these instances lead to the same outcome: imposter syndrome.

Because of this, even in business, I allowed a lot of people to take advantage of me because I did not value my own *opinion* and my own *insight* on things. I leaned toward other people, thinking they were smarter than me, and that created open doors for me to be taken advantage of. I *allowed* myself to overwork and to over-function because I didn't believe I was authentically good enough. I thought that I'd over-function to *prove* that I was good enough or to *prove* that I deserved a seat at the table. Imposter syndrome was a terrible thing for me, and it took a *long* time for me to work through it.

So *how* do you work through these twin pillars tearing down your self-image?

That's right, honey, we've talked about this before.

Survivor's guilt and imposter syndrome tie *back* to our self-worth.

And what have we said about self-worth? Lack of self-worth (even if you only feel it in a professional setting) opens you up to all *kinds* of ways to be hurt. We talked about how it commonly manifests as *people pleasing*, and guess what, that's *exactly* what we're talking about here! Giving in to requests, demands, pleas, to be someone else's come-up—those are *all* ways we people please as a way to compensate for our missing self-worth. It is the act of saying *yes* when we *really* want to say *no*. When we *deny* ourselves our own needs to make someone *else* happy. This can take place in your personal life or in your professional life. You know those people who are so eager to please at work, even though they *know* they're performing over their pay grade and being taken advantage of? Yep, that fits in here, too, with imposter syndrome and lack of self-worth.

Recall back in chapter 3 when we discussed how to go from people pleasing to pleasing *ourselves*. **First, find the root of your unresolved trauma.** What was the earliest memory in your life of being a people pleaser? Oftentimes it is rooted in some *practical* utility. It wasn't wrong to do it then.

Second, forgive yourself. You *were* a people pleaser. You can't change that from the past. So let it go.

Third, ask yourself how much wasted time and energy you've spent doing things you didn't want to do, all because you said *yes* to people when you needed to say no. Write them down so you can *see* them. See how long that list is.

Fourth, practice saying no as a complete sentence. In as few words as possible. You ain't being mean, you're just saying no. Figure out the *best* way to say no for you.

We can't let survivor's remorse hit us because we *don't* owe nobody *nothing*. The idea of feeling *guilt* over a come-up that was solely our own is *ridiculous*, and yet it is so prevalent in middle-class and lower-class families. It is so *easy* to fall into the trap of giving and taking care of others. Of course we want to help others, but we shouldn't have to rob ourselves to do so. I don't care if you're the nicest person out there, you *want* and *need* enough for yourself. That's just pure survival instinct. You have *got* to take care of yourself first—and *no*, you are *not* being selfish for looking out for number one.

Another way to look at it is to take the airplane analogy. If you've ever been on a plane, you've heard the pre-takeoff speech. It's always the same: *Put on your seat belt; have your seat back and tray table upright.* And what do they say when it comes to emergencies? If the oxygen levels drop and those masks pop down, you put your *own* oxygen mask on, *then* you assist those around you. If you're not breathing in the first place, how you gonna help someone else breathe? You're *dead*, baby!

The same goes for when you've got that extra money. You don't take care of yourself first, then you ain't gonna be able to help *anyone* else *anyway*. All you'll be doing is driving yourself to an early grave or early bankruptcy.

Acknowledge your past problems with self-worth, *own* them, then *change* them. Your image of self-worth *will* change in the process, and it is the *only* way you can learn to be unapologetic and protect yourself *and* your money.

Once you've taken the steps to understand and resolve your trauma around *why* you feel a lack of self-worth that leads you to people please through survivor's remorse and imposter syndrome, then you still gotta *address* the survivor's remorse and/or imposter syndrome itself. So, get in here and listen up!

The first step to addressing these twin beasts is to realize that you did what you needed to make yourself who you are *now*, and you don't owe anybody *anything*—especially if you know there's a good chance that their inability to *deal* with such gifts will bring *you* down in the process. If those around you are gonna reject your gifts, are gonna talk *shit* about them to make you feel like a fool, honey, say *goodbye*. Don't fuck with them no more!

What are you doing hanging around people who want to constantly put you down when you just *made* it? You deserve everything you got, and just because other people don't have what you have does *not* mean you should *give* it to them. Just because someone is in a situation that you *recognize*, that you *feel* because you used to be in that situation financially, emotionally, however you were in it, does *not* mean they automatically deserve your help. I don't give a damn *what* those rap songs say! It does *not* mean you automatically *need* to help them. It does *not* mean you need to feel *sorry* for them, and it does *not* mean you need to take *care* of them. *Absolutely*, you can be a resource for them. But you should not be *sacrificing* yourself just to get them to where you are.

Second, we must understand that people *are* where they are because of *themselves*. Yes, there are societal barriers that affect some more than others. I *ain't* denying that. Is there a certain amount of *luck* that can happen? Absolutely. But *ultimately*, people are where they are or they *stay* where they are because of their own choices. Once you realize that others are in the position they're in *because* of who they are and the choices that *they've* made, then the third step is to *accept* that they *also* have the ability to make the same choices you have. They have the *ability* to do what you've done; they've just chosen *not* to. And that is *not* your fault. You have done the work for yourself. You made different choices than they did, and you should not be feeling bad for them or feeling like you need to sacrifice yourself or over-function for someone who *chose* to not make those choices, and *continuously* chooses not to.

For me, I had to accept that I was not *any* luckier than anybody else. I made *choices* that other people didn't make. I made *sacrifices*. I went to a lot of different events to further myself that others wouldn't go to, wouldn't even *comprehend* going to. So when other people say to me, "You're just so lucky," I respond with, "If I'm so lucky, then why weren't you in the same rooms I was in? Why didn't you make the same sacrifices I was making? You can call me lucky when you do the *same* shit that I do, and you *don't* get the same outcome. But if you sat on the fucking sidelines, wishing and *hoping* for what I got, I'm *not* lucky. I just did what the fuck you *didn't* do."

The bottom line in these steps is that the only people who *deserve* your help are the people who are *ready* for your help. This is something I've learned through many broken hearts, having my feelings hurt and feeling *drained*. I'm trying to help y'all recognize this *before* you have to experience what I did, or if you are in the *middle* of this right now, to snap *out* of it.

The only people who *deserve* your help are the people who are *ready* for your help.

Your help is a *gift*. It is a *privilege* for people to get access to it. It is not something that everyone is *entitled* to. Just because you have identified their need, or their potential, does not mean *they* have identified the same things and are willing to *accept* your help.

Remember: Everyone is *not* your assignment.

Your assignment is the people who are ready to receive what you have to offer—and do the work *themselves* as opposed to waiting for you to save them. We have to realize that some people are just *happy* in their dysfunction. They have *accepted* the story of dysfunction in their lives. Is it unfortunate that they live that way? Absolutely. But is it *your* problem that they live that way? Absolutely *not*. Everybody's problem is not *your* problem.

I understand this is hard for those of us who grew up with helpers. It was hard for me, too, but we *got* to find that line, if only for our *own* sake. We cannot afford to be constantly drained. We should be helping those who want to help *themselves* first, so if someone is continuing to make poor choices in spite of the fact that they're *grown* and know they can make better choices, do *not* waste your time and energy on them. The Bible says, "Do not cast your pearls before swine." I'm not trying to call nobody pigs, but you don't give your good *stuff* to somebody who doesn't deserve it. Those are your jewels, and you don't want to spend them on someone who is *stuck* in a place of dysfunction *and* has no drive to get better. If they are *content* with where they are, living below their potential, that is *their* choice. Let them stay there until they realize and *want* to get better.

One last thing. I know this has been a ride, but I've got one more secret I want to share. Just because someone *says* they want to change does *not* mean they really are *ready* to change. You got a whole lot of people out here that have been singing the same song for a long time, and the reason they've been singing so long is because they don't actually want to change! They just want to make people, you included, *think* they're gonna change because it softens people up toward them. Just like *you* can see their potential, *they* can see that helping spirit within you, and they will tell you whatever you need to hear just to keep you *around.* They're like *vampires.* They are gonna suck your energy dry from you contributing to them without them pouring anything *out* of themselves or back into you. They ain't making no changes, they just like having that good help and spirit around, and they will talk up a huge game of what they're gonna do, of what they *plan* to do. But here's the secret to the sauce:

If they're not actually *making* those steps, then they're not about the business of change.

Until someone takes the action to *improve* their life, that person is not ready to *change* their life. You need to accept the *truth* of the fact that if they *wanted* to do differently, they *would* be doing differently. And it wouldn't change just because *you* or someone else they knew had a recent come-up and can now *help* them out of that situation. Look for that when these folks or whoever come up, dragging along that pile of bullshit that is survivor's remorse. Because that *is* the secret to the sauce. That will help you *discern* between the people who really want to change and those who just want what you can give them without doing a damn thing to improve themselves.

Realize, understand, and accept. These steps will help y'all to no longer hang with survivor's remorse. Don't let nobody guilt you about where you're at, or come at you with none of that "must be nice to be where you are" shit. And if they do, be *honest*! Yes, it is absolutely *wonderful.* I *love* where I'm at. They ain't gonna like that one bit, ooh, I can tell you now, but who fucking cares? They might call you snobby and all them nasty names, but, listen, they could have done the same. They have their own ability to manifest what they wanted, and they did *not. You* did. And just because you are *enjoying* the benefits of that, of taking your life to the next level and making the sacrifices you did, does *not* mean you are being snobby. It does *not.*

If people want to *know* how I got to where I'm at, I will *gladly* show and tell them, but I am not gonna *bring* them here. Just because I don't handhold them through the whole thing does *not* mean I am not here for them. I am just not *willing* to use my abundance to make them feel like *they* live the lifestyle that they ain't *worked* for. That is *toxic.* That don't help nobody. It does not help me because it *drains* my resources, and it does not help them because it does not *teach* them anything.

What I advocate for, especially when it's someone trying to help out their mom, dad, brother, sister, cousin, aunt, or other family member, is *balance.* If this person is someone *you* have decided is worth having in your life, then you need to have a *balanced* approach to their come-up and your role in that. Set a budget. Have an honest conversation. Set your *boundaries* and stick to them. And if it's family, yes, you may need to rinse and repeat more often than you'd like before they get the message.

Realize your own hard work, accept that you deserve to be *exactly* where you are, and *distance* yourself from anybody who treats you otherwise. You are worth *more* than that, and let me tell you, there ain't *no* shame in reminding yourself of that. Remind yourself when you don't believe it, and eventually you *will.*

Take Action to Get the F*ck Out Your Own Way

If you're always feeling guilty that you have more and are trying to be other people's come-ups, try these steps the next time you want to cave in to someone's request:

Take a look at your own self-worth. Refer back to chapter 3 to go from people pleasing to pleasing yourself.

Find the root of your unresolved trauma.

Forgive yourself.

Make a list of all the times you've pleased others to the DETRIMENT of yourself.

Practice saying no as a complete sentence.

Once you've worked through your self-worth issues, now it's time to put your skills to the test. The next time you get triggered when someone asks for help–someone who does NOTHING to help themselves–remember these rules:

Realize that you deserve everything you have–you worked for it, nobody else did.

Understand that others are where they are because of the choices they have made and accept that they STILL have the option to make better choices if THEY choose to. Their problem is not always your problem.

Accept that they CAN change, they just choose not to. You can guide them and tell them how you got where you are, but you cannot be their piggy bank. Do not let them bleed you dry.

Talk yourself up in your vulnerable moments. Self-talk is a powerful tool, and it is something that helped me tremendously in overcoming survivor's guilt and imposter syndrome. So, remind yourself of how hard you worked and how you deserve to be where you are–literally say it to yourself every time you start to have an idea to the contrary. Chile, every time!

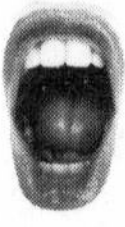

15

Stop Being So Needy

We've talked a *lot* about self-worth and feeling secure in yourself—within your *full* self—and about the many awful behaviors and tendencies that come out of having insecurities, but, baby, you *know* I got more to say on the matter, and here it is: To all the needy folks out there, *stop being so damn needy all the time.* Get in here, get in here, get *in* here! Y'all know about them Negative Nancys. But do you know them *Needy* Nancys? You might know one! We're gonna figure that out today. Because y'all have chosen to get your shit together and get out of your own way, so come in real close. We gotta understand what it *means* to be needy.

But first, I'm gonna talk about it in the context of something y'all usually come to me *for*, and that is y'all's *relationships.* Most people, when they hear the word "needy," jump immediately to relationships because they probably *know* someone, or they *are* that someone, that others complain about being too fucking needy. *He needs this, that, blah blah blah, she won't give me no time of the day if I'm not with her every fucking second,* and so on and so on. In the *context* of relationships, being needy is when y'all are depending on someone else to *emotionally* provide for you what you *should* be providing for yourself. When you don't, you end up having an *insatiable* appetite. You are *depending* on someone else to fill an emotional void that *only* you can fill. *That* is why the appetite is insatiable—if the void *could* be filled by someone else, it would have! You would've gotten what you needed, and you would have *stopped* being so needy once you got it. But because this void can only be filled by *you,* other people ain't gonna cut it.

Needy people have an endless appetite. No matter *how* much is given to them, they *still* want more. They want what *they* can and *should* give *themselves,* but they're so stuck in their self-delusion that they can't see for themselves that they should be fulfilling their *own* emotional need for time and attention, and they latch on to *others* for this instead. Self-delusion means the *failure to recognize reality.* In other words, you can't *see* that the reality of the situation is that you *are* a needy person and that it's *not* anyone else's responsibility to fulfill the time and attention needs *for* you.

We're gonna *end* that delusion right here, right now. Walk with me, baby, and let's see what this neediness behavior looks like. Don't you run away if the image gets too familiar for you—uh-uh, that's not what we do. We face it, we *own* it, and we work through that shit.

Neediness in a person means needing *affirmation.* Affirmation is gonna look different for everyone, but it is a *pattern* of always needing some kind of affirmation from others that separates someone who's *perpetually* needy from someone who might just be feeling needy *temporarily.* If you're just feeling needy about one thing every blue moon—maybe you need someone to lean on after a bad breakup, and after a few weeks, you're *good* to carry on—that ain't being a Needy Nancy. But if you *constantly* need someone's time or attention directed at you all the time, baby, you might have a neediness problem.

We *see* neediness in others; in fact, we are fucking *good* at spotting when others are needy. But we can't always see it in *ourselves.* Just like everything else we've talked about so far, from owning your shit to being emotionally unavailable to top drawering yourself, we can be *awful* at recognizing what's already in us.

If you are emotionally *triggered* each time you feel someone is not giving you enough attention, then that's something to take a look at. If you *feel* like you are walking a fucking *tight*rope around other people because you always calculating how much time they spend with you, look at that. If you see within your relationship patterns the trend that it's *hard* for other people to ever give you *enough* attention, pay attention to that. I know we all *hate* looking back on our old relationships, *hate* thinking about our exes and whatever, but let me tell you, you can learn *a lot* about yourself from your relationship patterns.

If it's *hard* for you to continually find someone that can give you enough *time* and *attention*, you might be the needy one! If you get upset over somebody who normally *does* spend a reasonable amount of time with you not being available for some legitimate reason, you might be needy. If you've got no sense of *flexibility*, if you are *rigid* about time like, "You *need* to spend time with me"; no, I don't *care* if you ain't seen your mother in however long, girl, you might be needy. If you're somebody who puts very, very *restrictive* timelines on text responses or electronic communication responses, you might be needy. Let's elaborate on that for a moment here.

This situation with *texting* has gotten way out of hand, if you ask me. *I text you all the time, why don't you text me back? Why it take you this many hours to text me back? What you doing, and who you doing it with? Huh? Huh?*

That shit right there.

This is a *huge* and *common* form of neediness that I see, that I get messages about all the *time*! I have *seen* it repeatedly: People stop dating someone because of how that other person approaches texting. And that's just silly—no, it is! Y'all don't *need* to be breaking up over shit like this. It is *stupid*, and I'm about to tell you why.

People communicate at different speeds and in different

ways all the damn time; this ain't some new revelation. The reality *is* that some people—and I'm one of those people—*literally* don't text anyone back immediately. For example, I'm one of those people who literally don't text anyone back immediately *unless* you are one of my kids or an *immediate* family member. That's it. That's part of my *parental* responsibility. That's part of my *familial* responsibility. *Outside* of that, I will text you back (a) when I *have* the information to text you back with, (b) when I've had time to *process* the text message, or (c) when I'm *ready* to start a conversation with you. Because maybe I *know* you text back very quickly and I don't want to start a conversation at that moment, so I see the message and I go, "Oh, okay, cool. I'll text back later." I ain't trying to get that going right now, and that is *okay*.

It's *okay* to not respond right away! If that ain't your communication style, then don't feel obligated to do anything else but what is comfortable for *you* and what is right for *you* in that moment. So if *I'm* not comfortable responding to your every text within five minutes, I ain't *going* to! I will *not* switch around the way I've communicated my whole life *just* because someone else *expects* me to.

Neediness comes down to when we're *expecting* other people's communication patterns to *match* and *mimic* our own. And on that note, I have something to say to each one of you checking your phone every thirty seconds for that text from that someone you're so desperately hanging on to. I don't care if it's your partner, your friend, your family member—whoever it is, y'all need to hear this:

For the sake of *your* mental health, *stop* taking it so personal every single time that someone you know, you love, you like, doesn't contact you back as quickly as you like. Or for that matter, they don't contact you back at *all*!

People go through things, and sometimes it's a lot of stuff that you don't know *anything* about. When people are going through things, they are just trying to use that *little* bit of energy they got to get through what they trying to get through. You being in their life may certainly be something that they *value*, and they *want* to be in communication with you, but sometimes they just don't have that energy to *give*. So *stop* taking it personal. *Stop* sending those text messages of, *Hey stranger, ain't heard from you in a while*—stop guilting them! Instead, reach out to them and say, *Hey, I know you may be going through things right now, not sure what's going on in your life, just sending you love. Reach out whenever you're ready, no pressure.* Be a *support* system, not a source of *guilt*, and stop taking things personal that have *nothing* to do with you!

Just because someone has not responded to you in five, ten, thirty minutes, or even six fucking hours does *not* mean they don't care about you. It does *not* mean they hate you or do not want to be in your life anymore. You gotta know when to press and when to back off, and I'm telling you right now, most of the time you gotta back *off*. They don't have the energy, plain and simple, and that should be respected.

When they *don't* feel respected and you send a million more messages prodding and poking them to respond, how *do* you expect them to respond? What makes you think they will *want* to respond after all that? You just sent them the *biggest* fucking red flag in the universe, and if they're keeping their eyes open, they will be running for the hills. And I can't blame them. Their boundaries were just stepped all over, disrespected, ignored, and who would want to stay in that sort of relationship?

Neediness doesn't end with romantic relationships. It happens in friendships, too, and I bet y'all know or you might *be* that one emotional *vampire* in the friend group. It's that person who will call at any time, who will talk nonstop, no one else can get a *word* in, and then they wonder why other people don't pick up when they call! It's because they *drain* them, baby! They are *draining*. People might love them to death, but they are *draining*. This is the friend where everybody in the friend group knows what *that* person is going through, but they don't know what's going on in *anyone* else's life because the needy friend is too busy calling them up and unpacking *their* shit onto everyone else.

"Oh, boo, we should go out to lunch soon."

No, boo, I don't wanna go out to lunch with you! Lunch with you means I will be sitting there like your therapist with you *pouring* things onto me. Here's the thing: As your friend, I am here to be in your corner, but my expectation is that you will also be in *my* corner. And that the love and support that I'm giving you, you will give *back* to me.

I'm telling you this because if you are this person, know that your friends may not tell you this. What they *will* tell you is "Girl, I'm busy, I'll call you back soon!" or "Bro, I hope you're doing good, we're gonna catch up soon!" Or you talk to them and all they say is "That's what's up."

When someone says, "That's what's up," what they're really saying is "You are *draining* me. I'm not paying attention, and I'm hoping that this is the last statement you will make because I'm ready for this conversation to be done." Don't be that friend, honey. Don't put your friends through that, because I *guarantee* they will not be in your life for much longer. Your *neediness* is gonna drive them away, and lemme tell you something, one of the *quickest* ways someone can escort themselves out of my life is to constantly ask me for advice whenever we sit down together. I know, giving advice is what I *do*, but does that mean I want to be doing that twenty-four seven? Hell no! I *know* what my boundaries are, and some of y'all don't know yours, but do you see the pattern here with neediness? It is a blatant *disregard* for other people's boundaries that perpetually needy folk are prone to doing. I ain't here to diagnose, but y'all know my past relationship patterns and y'all know the type of men I used to date, and lemme just say that there is also a slight seasoning of narcissism in neediness, along with that inability to fulfill their own needs.

It may be slight, but it's there.

It's the idea that *they* exist at the center of the motherfucking universe. And if other people don't treat them in the way *they* see themselves, then that's when the meltdown happens.

It happens when things don't go their *way*.

When you don't text back right away. When you gotta *work* late. When you can't spend the evening with them because you have prior plans or something unexpected came up. Meltdowns happen, they go off on people, and relationships end.

Here's the secret when it comes to knowing what neediness looks like. You have a legitimate reason for not being able to spend time with them. You've made it clear. You've *told* them in advance. You've let them know what you can and can't do in that moment, and what do they do? They *ignore* you. They *disregard* your request and your boundaries. They *inundate* you with their *own* requests and demands, and every time they poke at you, you feel that *fear* underneath it all that can turn to explosive anger at the drop of a hat. *That's* what neediness looks like.

So now we know what neediness *is* and what it *looks* like. But just like every other self-worth topic in this book, we gotta understand *why* people are needy to a hurtful degree. I'll *tell* you why. Come on in, nice and close. *Most* people who are needy are like that—unable to fulfill their own emotional needs and leaning on others to do so, along with a little narcissism—because their neediness is based in past unresolved trauma. Sound familiar? I hope so! But I'm gonna tell you what I've seen as some of the root causes of neediness. Maybe you'll recognize them, maybe they'll set off a spark in your mind.

Number one is *abandonment* issues. Issues where you have a deep *fear* that people are gonna *leave* you, that no one's gonna *stay*. And that can so *easily* be turned into neediness; if someone close to them is away for too long, maybe they just went on a two-week vacation across the world—that could *trigger* their abandonment. Even if they *know* the return date, in their mind, they might twist it in a way that makes them think they don't *really* know, that they can't *rely* on that given date to hold up. Or maybe that person has been lying all along and is really out doing something they shouldn't be doing. Remember those stories we tell ourselves? That comes into play here with abandonment issues and neediness as well.

The core of abandonment issues is this: You gotta recognize that whatever abandonment happened to you before happened in the *past*, and it's *not* reflective of what's gonna always happen in the future. At the end of the day, it's you realizing that not everyone is gonna abandon you. And what helps you realize that is to recognize that *you* deserve to have people around you and that you are *likable*—and if you're not likable, then be fucking honest with yourself and *work* on that shit! Look back at the previous chapters from the beginning of this book. I talk all day and *night* about owning your shit, working through generational trauma or trauma of any type, and cultivating a *better* self-esteem that allows who you truly *are* to shine through.

The second root cause of abandonment issues is a need for *control*. People who suffer from control issues think that they will *avoid* being hurt if they control everything that's happening. If I can make sure you call me back in this much time, if you operate in the way that I want you to operate, then I'm *cutting* off the opportunity for you to be in communication with other people, I'm *cutting* off the opportunity for you to go and do something I don't like, and I'm *cutting* off the opportunity for you to just simply fall out of love with me. I control *everything*, so whatever I want to have happen *will* happen. That's what a needy person whose neediness is built on control issues will do. They're gonna try to control *everything* so that they can control the outcome. But here's the *problem*. I've *yet* to see a needy person build a healthy relationship or get the commitment they're truly looking for out of anyone. It actually produces the *opposite* outcome. It *destroys* your relationships. It *erodes* trust and it *pushes* people away. And these people, they *never* see it coming, so they never *think* that it's their controlling that is the problem. That lack of awareness and *overabundance* of self-delusion allows the cycle to repeat.

Number three is *trust* issues. Say you had a parent who never trusted you, who would turn your room inside out on a daily basis *because* they didn't trust you, which in turn now feeds your current behavior and thought patterns. Imagine you're with a partner who has given you absolutely no fucking reason to think they may be cheating. But there's an insecurity within you that says otherwise. So you violate their privacy. It starts small, maybe checking their phone. Looking into their social media accounts for any fucking around in the DMs. That could even turn into you *stalking* them when they leave the house to catch up with a friend. But my point is that, outside the obvious that you are poking your nose into places it don't belong and violating both their privacy *and* their trust, you are also creating an *addiction.*

There is an addictive *quality* to snooping, to neediness. Why do we snoop and search? To get comfort, affirmation, and *know* what's going on. But what we don't realize is that nothing is gonna be able to satisfy our search because these insecurities stem from *within* us, not from whatever's in that phone or DM. You're gonna go to more and more extraordinary *lengths* to be able to be affirmed or *pacified* for a temporary time. That's how neediness can become a slippery slope that can ruin your relationships.

Because neediness comes from unresolved trauma, you know by now what y'all's first step is gonna be. Take *away* its power by *owning* it.

First, you have to truly understand if you *are* needy, or if someone you know is needy. And if it's still not clear to you from the examples I've given here whether you're needy or not, then just ask. If you real big and bold, just *ask* someone—a trusted friend or family member who *knows* you and ain't afraid to spit some truths and who does not have negative intentions toward you.

Neediness occurs in every facet of our lives, not just relationships! Some people are needy with their spouse, some are needy with their kids, with their parents, with their friends, with their *family*. So ask the people you trust, who *don't* have a history of saying things to be harmful to you. If you *suspect* yourself of being needy, ask the people close to you: "On a scale from zero to ten, how needy do you think I am? Zero being not at all, ten being the highest." Let them answer. Don't interrupt them or guide them in any way after asking. Ask the damn question, and then close your mouth. Ask them to be *completely* honest and be open to the answer. *Don't* criticize them or get mad at them if their answer is not what you like.

Say they come back to you with their answer, and it's a nine. Then what? The second step is to figure out what the root cause of *your* neediness is. Is it abandonment issues, control issues, trust issues? The easiest way to think about this is to ask yourself what your deepest *fear* is. Not your deepest fear in general, but what fears come to mind when you think about *not* being in *control*, or being *abandoned*, or someone not *contacting* you.

Be *honest* with yourself about those fears. Remember that you are *removing* shame from them by acknowledging what they are. It may be painful in the moment, but once you sit with them and realize that you *have* them, they'll have less control over you and the less *powerful* they will become. The pain you feel then will be nothing compared to the pain you'd *continue* to feel if you ignored your cause of neediness.

Once you've sat with your pain and absorbed it, *felt* it, and worked through it to the other side by letting those emotions wash over you without trying to run away from them, now you gotta let that shit *go.* Search your memory bank for the *earliest* occurrence of your deepest fear. Where were you? How old were you? Who else was *involved* in that situation? What happened? And what you'll realize is that the fears that are currently *driving* your neediness were *created* by those experiences you recall now. They were created by things that happened long *before* the people who are currently in your life were there.

Once y'all are able to identify the *source* and initial *moment* of your neediness, that will help you to be able to see that *this person who I'm being so clingy with didn't create the issue. Therefore, why am I expecting their actions to be able to fix this issue?*

Neediness comes from *us.* Which means it can only be *fixed* by us. *That's* how you learn to let that shit go. If y'all take nothing else away from this chapter, then let it be this: *No one* else can affirm you enough to make you feel secure.

No one.

I do not care how *much* information they give you. I do not care if they answer *every single call.* I do not care if they're *available* to you twenty-four hours out of the day! *None* of that will make you feel more secure. It will only *pacify* you in that moment because your *fears* that are driving your neediness are *bigger* than that. So there's *nothing* anyone else can do about it, and that's what kills relationships. You ever heard a partner say, or someone say about their partner, "I do *everything* you want. I do *everything*—and you're still not happy. What else can I do?"

Nothing, honey. You can do absolutely nothing else. Or you can do more if you don't like that answer, but nothing will change.

Then you'll be back here wondering, *Is anything ever enough?*

The answer is no. People get exhausted and they leave. And then the needy person doesn't understand that they exhaust the *fuck* out of people. What's more is that until they *do* look within themselves and follow the steps above, they will *continue* to exhaust every partner, friend, and family member they have. And some of those relationships will never recover.

This insatiable pit we call neediness, this *need* for affirmation, all comes back to the fact that you are not yet your true self. Your full self. You won't be your *full* self until you have *accepted* all your past trauma. Until you've done the work to feel it, sit with it, and then let go of that trauma. If that pit is already filled by you, then you're able to come into your relationships and friendships *whole*. When you haven't done that, you end up being needy. You end up asking someone else to fill you up, to validate you, to prop you up, to affirm you—all while shirking your own damn responsibility to affirm yourself!

Girl, that ain't *right*.

You are putting an unnecessary burden and fatigue on others because you are too *selfish* and *afraid* of confronting yourself, your demons, your trauma, so you would rather run others headfirst into the ground. This issue starts and *ends* with you, honey. Don't be bringing anyone else into the picture until you've worked through what's happening within *you*.

Take Action to Get the F*ck Out Your Own Way

Are you needy? If you're unsure, ask someone you trust, "On a scale of zero to ten, how needy do you think I am?"

Next, identify your deepest fears. Ask yourself what comes to mind when you think about not being in control, of someone not contacting you, etc. What fears do you have?

Last, search your memory. What is the earliest memory you have of experiencing that pain or fear? Allow yourself to sit with it, then let it go.

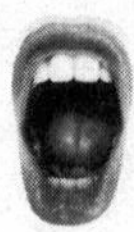

16

Stop Trying to Fit In

Insecurity and low self-worth lead to people being Needy Nancys, but lemme just say, that ain't the *only* negative behavior to come out of these messy baskets of life. Get in here, baby, because we're gonna talk about fitting *in.* That hot topic seems to never go away no matter how old you get.

Being needy means wanting and *expecting* other people to mimic and match what *you* want, but wanting to fit in flips the script. Wanting to fit in is about undervaluing your own *uniqueness* through trying to mimic and match *other people.* It is when *you* change what you *do,* what you *want,* maybe even what you *think* and *believe,* to match someone else or some group.

There are *over* eight *billion* people on the face of the earth. *Being consumed* with trying to fit in with a specific group of people is just a fucking waste of *time*. Our journey is about becoming our *full* self because when we are our full self, we *attract* people who are like us. Therefore, trying to fit in no longer is an *issue* because people who are like us will *gravitate* toward us. So, just like with being needy, wanting to fit in is a reflection of your insecurity. It's the idea of *I'm not good enough, and I will be validated or feel good enough once this particular group lets me in with them.*

The characteristics that come with this type of thought pattern often revolve around what we *wear*. You might see everything you *wear* as a reflection of what you've seen other people wear. But does it look nice because *you* actually think it looks nice—or that it would look nice on you and *your* body type—or does it look nice because you've seen somebody *else* wear it who you admire? Most of the time, people who want to fit in will never ask themselves that question. It won't even cross their *minds* because they're too busy getting whatever it is they *think* they need to fit in. But that's one of the biggest characteristics of anyone looking to fit in: that they *choose* what they do and don't do based on what they see *other* people doing. They are *obsessed* with how other people view them. They are not *listening* to their own internal compass, or, in some cases, their internal compass is bent all out of whack and is based on what they see other people doing. Take it from me because it wasn't long ago that I *finally* stopped trying to fit in.

Y'all know I've never fit in since my childhood. A shy, gay

Black boy growing up in the South? Ain't *nothing* about me fit in anywhere, and I knew it. I tried like no other to fit in with various different groups at school. There was always some group or other that I was trailing, nipping at them heels to get them to pay me some attention. That was me in high school, in college, and in my twenties. I wanted to fit in. I *wanted* to be invited to the parties and events. There was always *something* else I was striving to be, and I spent so much time, energy, and money on all of that. It was *exhausting.*

The biggest reason why folks try to fit in is because they're surrounded by people who make them feel like they're not enough. If you're *not* like them, you get *judged.* And I'm gonna share a little story from my *own* experience. We might *have* good reasons for wanting to fit in—for opportunities, to make *friends*—but no matter *how* good your reasons are, the only thing that really matters is that by doing so, you aren't operating in your *authentic* self.

No matter *what* your reason is for wanting to fit in, ask yourself *why* you are willing to let *them* tell you when, where, and how you're worth something. Go ahead, ask! That's what I did, and lemme tell you, I could not come up with a single goddamn reason why. And that's when I decided that I was no longer gonna give other people the authority to validate my self-worth. That's when I *freed* myself to *be* my full self. It was scary at first. I had fears and worries, but I also had *faith* and *confidence* in my talents. In my *work.* The key to my success is *not* in trying to fit in. It is in my accepting the *goodness* and *greatness* of who *I* am, and then figuring out what's the best path forward from there.

When I decided I was gonna build a business around being my full self, letting my talent for talking lead the way, I had to make a lot of changes to the videos I was doing. I said, *I'm gonna stop doing these pretty little videos all the time.* Go look back at my old videos and see for yourself. I used to sit back with one leg crossed over the other, hands on top of each other placed neatly on my knee, back straight, and I'd sit there on camera and never raise my voice—*fuck* that. I'm not doing that no more. If I want to show a little more of my collarbone, if I wanna put my sweats on, I'm gonna be *me*.

And you know what happened once I did that?

The views went *up*. They went up from one million a month to two million a month to *ten* million a month just on Facebook *alone*. It was so *crazy*, and here's the thing, y'all. My follower numbers might be lower than those of many public figures, but my *views* are off the charts! And you know why? It's because I can be myself. I can talk to *you* directly and ask for shares, for likes, and bless y'all, you keep sharing the videos! All those shares add up, and I reach tons of people every day, and my platform is growing. And as it's growing, I make more money and more products. I am *accumulating* more with my core competencies and unique-abilities. And the thing about being myself, my *full* self, is that if you watch me online, there's probably no one else you've ever seen like me. If I'd taken the platform those executives were offering me, that *Queer Eye* idea, for example, baby, I wouldn't have been me. I wouldn't have been *happy*, and I wouldn't have been living my best life.

If you're wondering if I'm living my best life, lemme tell you something. People come up to me on a regular basis and ask me, "Do you want to be on TV?"

I say, "That'd be cute, but, baby, I'm making more than half the people I know *on* TV, just sitting here on this little iPhone. And guess what? I ain't got to *audition* for shit, I ain't got to wait on people to tell me yes—I'm my *own* motherfucking yes!"

I ain't trying to speak down or look down on nobody. If a TV show wants me and calls me for a part, I'm gonna do it. But my point is this: Trying to fit in will fuck you up. It will fuck you up because while you're trying to fit in, what you're really doing is missing out on your own greatness, baby. Whatever you *are*, whatever you *do*, find the light and beauty in that. After you find your light and your beauty, what I want you to do is to only focus on what you can do to manifest that. What can you do to illuminate the greatness in that? Don't try to fit in with nobody else, because you are losing who you are in the process. If I had continued to try to fit in with everybody else, I would not be sitting in the position I'm sitting in today.

I live a good life, baby. These cute pedicured toes don't touch the bare floor of my bedroom until at least 10:30 every morning. I don't have to get up early. I ain't got to audition for nobody to tell me yes; I'm my only yes. I make great money, I take care of my family, and I live a great life. It's because I don't try to fit in no more. I'm just me, and that's why y'all love me. I'm real, I'm authentic, and I live a wonderful, blessed life as a result. I encourage you to do the same.

So, darling, your circumstance might be different, but I *promise* you that fitting in is *not* the way to get better. And if you're someone trying to fit in, this is what you can do to fix it.

There's a question we never ask ourselves when we're trying so desperately to fit in, and it's a question that can *literally* lift a blindfold off your eyes. It can *shake* the self-delusion off of you. I *wish* I had asked myself this, or that someone had asked me this, because it would have *forced* me to think deeper on the issue.

Why don't I fit in with this group in the first place? Why am I not being invited into the circle as aggressively as I see other people being invited in?

Go on and ask! And what you might see is an answer we've talked about before. Just like when you get ghosted, just like when that somebody breaks up with you out of nowhere when you thought y'all were in sync, the *same* goes for when you're running yourself *ragged* trying to fit in. Sometimes when you *can't* fit in with the group or you feel like someone's *blocking* you from fitting in, you're actually being protected from all that comes with that group. It might be that these other people see that y'all got nothing in common before *you* do. They see you, and they know you not gonna be about the fuck shit they about, like, *I can tell by looking at you, it's not gonna be a good fit.* They just *know*, and their actions are gonna reflect it. So if you've been trying for weeks, for *months*, to fit in and no one giving you the time of day, ask yourself why. It's not because you're not trying hard enough. It's because they've seen who you are and they *know* who they are, and those two don't mix. Y'all might hate to hear this, but they are *protecting* you in a way, and you just gotta accept it and move on. You are *good* as you are, but you're just *not* a good fit *there*.

Often what happens in this case is that after we've been *removed* from the situation, we start to see *how* we've been protected. When I was trying so hard to fit in with those TV personalities and producer folk, it wasn't until *after* I'd made changes to my videos and started seeing the rewards of that that I began to see the cracks in their stuff. They were into fuck *shit* with those ideas. I didn't want no part in that. So I was *glad*, after the fact, after the pain, that it happened the way it happened.

Ask yourself *why* you don't fit in, and then ask yourself how *comfortable* you are with what you're doing to try to fit in. These decisions you're making in terms of what you got to do to fit in—maybe it's down to how you *dress*, where you *go*, or even what you *think* about yourself—are those 100 percent shaped by *you*, or are they shaped by what you want other people to *believe* about you? And are you *comfortable* doing those things or do they give you some odd feeling?

Sometimes it ain't a matter of them rejecting you, it's a matter of *you* struggling to feel comfortable around a group. Pay *attention* to that. Our first instincts are a *compass* for what's healthy for us in a lot of cases. So if you consistently feel a discomfort around a certain group that you really wanna try to fit into, or you don't feel like it's a *natural* fit with the group, *pay attention to that.* Because the things that work for us often have *flow* and *ease* attached to them. So if you're struggling to fit in with a specific group, you need to pay attention to that and not *ignore* what you're feeling.

So how do we *stop* this behavior? This comes back to self-esteem. So *many* of our personal issues come from lack of self-esteem, so are you gonna face it head-on, or are you gonna let it dominate your life and let it ruin your chance at living your *best* life? You can't *appreciate* the uniqueness of who you are if you don't *honor* the uniqueness of who you are first. And in order to *honor* your uniqueness, you need to surround yourself with people who make you feel like you are *good enough* as you are—even if that means having very *few* people around you, initially, who make you feel *honored* for who you actually *are*. Because if you're around people who make you feel less than that, that's only gonna hurt you. It *is* hurting you. Why are you around those people? Why are you *keeping* them in your life?

That's your next step: to be *honest* with yourself about what you actually like. In order to do that, you have to take a look at your feelings. I know feelings are not *facts*, but that don't mean they can't tell you anything, either. Feelings are *incredibly* helpful in letting you identify what it is you do and do not like. You may be wearing the clothes that everybody else wears, you may be *going* to all the hip places people go, you may be doing all this cool *stuff* everyone is doing, but how are you *feeling*? You might *look* great, but if you're still miserable, clearly that's not *enough.* Ask yourself this: *What would make* me *happy?*

This is a *revolutionary* question, which is just awful that we've never been asked or we've never given ourselves permission to ask before. But I'm telling you to do it now and do it for real.

What would make *me* happy?

Despite what everyone else is doing, *despite* what everyone else thinks, *despite* what the crowd or my family or my culture is doing, what would make *me* happy?

Write it down—and if your list looks like a bunch of superficial shit (a new house, more trips, or new clothes would make me happy), then you may have to scratch that list and start over again because money-based shit ain't gonna make nobody happy to their core long term. Your happiness has to come from *inside* you first. Put your list somewhere where you can see it every day and remember that what you're doing is the best for *you.* Having that time and space for yourself can be very *helpful* in seeing your value.

The *last* thing I want y'all to do is *tell* yourself you are enough. When you realize you are good enough, it will set the stage for you to have peace with who you are, so you can *illuminate* within that path and just live within the essence of your design.

Knowing you are enough, that you have talent, that you have

work ethic, that you *yourself* can make things happen that bring out the *best* in you and the best *for* you, will allow you to make decisions you never allowed yourself to dream before because you *knew* they would upset him, her, or them. You *knew* it would piss your parents off if you moved across the state. You *knew* it would make your best friend sad if you quit the job you had with her to move to another company. *Whatever* it is, knowing you are enough will give you the *freedom* to pursue those things. Things that maybe you always wanted but never did for fear of *judgment*, of *losing* your friends, of *ostracizing* someone or some group.

But you're not doing that anymore!

I spoke about my move to Bali earlier but let me just reiterate it here. That was the fucking *epitome* of not trying to fit in! Who the *fuck* is getting up and leaving Los Angeles County to move to Indonesia? Well, sweetie, *I* am. You know why? Because I gotta do what is right for *me*. What I wanted was peace and less pressure, so I had to make a choice to do what *I* wanted even if it made no sense to anyone else. And I honored myself because *I am enough*.

You. Are. *Enough*.

Ask yourself what would make *you* happy right now and create a path to get it. It might include doing something or multiple somethings that don't even make *sense* to other people. As long as you ain't hurting nobody or breaking no law, *go* for it. The key to honoring yourself is to be *willing* to do things that don't make sense to other people as long as it works for *you*. *That* is how you honor yourself. Once you start down the trajectory that illuminates your full self, you will *never* go back to wanting to fit in with a group that doesn't match who you are and who you want to be.

So, say it again.

I. Am. *Enough.*

Take Action to Get the F*ck Out Your Own Way

If you find yourself always trying to get IN with some other group, take a step back and ask yourself these questions:

Why don't I fit in with this group in the first place?

Why am I not being invited into the circle as aggressively as I see other people being invited in?

Sometimes, you're simply being protected. Maybe this group realizes that you two ain't a good fit, and while that's a tough pill to swallow, realize that in the long term, it will BENEFIT you. Being in the group ain't you. With that said, ask yourself this:

How COMFORTABLE am I with doing the things I'm doing to fit in?

If you feel anything is off, here's your next step:

Ask yourself, *What would make ME happy?* Do it for real. Despite everything and everybody else, what would make ME happy? Then create your path to get there, DESPITE what everyone and everything in your life is telling you. Turn a blind eye and a deaf ear to everything else because they don't matter when it comes to figuring out how to make YOU happy.

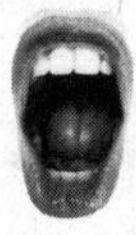

17

Am I an Asshole?

When we choose to give others our guidebook, choose *ourselves* over others, and act in the way that allows our full selves to take form, we are gonna encounter nagging questions that will attempt to turn us around. We're about to discuss the mother of *all* such questions right here, right now.

Am I an asshole?

Here's the thing, baby. Now that we've *learned* how to choose ourselves in so many different facets of life, it feels *good* to choose yourself, but making those decisions and *sticking* to them is gonna pave the way for this question to come snapping at your heels. It *will* come to you, I can promise you that. But I'm gonna show you how to deal with it and *not* let it make you backpedal so that your insecurities start showing up again. Get in here and squeeze close!

Let's start with rephrasing this question. When others cause you to start *thinking* you might be an asshole just because you've learned to put up your own healthy boundaries like you never did or could before, turn this question around on yourself like this: *Do I have asshole tendencies?* In other words, do you have traits that you believe are protecting you but that are actually *produced* by bitterness?

I'm gonna answer for you. *Yes.* We *all* have these tendencies. Whether or not we *acknowledge* them is another question. These traits oftentimes *come* from healthy desires, like the desire to be validated or *seen* for who our authentic selves are—that's great, that's what we *want*! But it ain't giving you the license to let past bitterness rear its ugly head to make you an asshole. If these traits manifest themselves in ugly, selfish ways with no tact for anybody else, *that's* where the issue of you being an asshole might come into play.

We all have asshole tendencies. Some may have disproportionately more, such as with a narcissist. But the difference between being an asshole and protecting yourself is that protecting yourself (your self-worth, your happiness, your inner peace, and your time) means drawing healthy boundaries between you and ill treatment. Being an asshole, on the other hand, comes from a place of bitterness and inner anger that you haven't dealt with yet. Take note when those ugly feelings rear their heads because that means it's time to work *through* that shit!

We gotta be *honest* with ourselves about the fact that there are parts of us that may *rub* people the wrong way, *but* also be clear with ourselves that just because they rub someone the wrong way doesn't mean there's always something wrong with those traits. Let me give you an example.

Y'all know I am *comfortable* with who I am. And that trait allows me to be very transparent. In every video I have, I am past the moon and *back* with my transparency. You've *felt* it through my videos. My transparency will rub somebody the wrong way if they're not comfortable with who *they* are. But that doesn't mean there's anything *wrong* with my transparency. I ain't doing nothing to hurt someone else. *That's* the difference between knowing if a trait is bad or not. If you are operating authentically, and it doesn't negatively affect anybody, but people just don't *like* it, you are not being an asshole. Me being authentically *myself* in my videos and telling y'all what I think about a particularly divisive topic and someone not *liking* what I'm saying don't make *me* an asshole. It don't make *them* an asshole, either, maybe just an insecure person who can't see that who *I* am has nothing to do with them. I'm just being authentic. And they are being authentic not liking what I'm saying and that's *fine*. Now, if they went all over my videos posting hate comments or sending me letters or emails *expressing* that hate and viscerally trying to *hurt* me in that way, then, yes, they *are* an asshole, which brings me to my next differentiating point.

An asshole trait is when you are *doing* things *knowing* that it hurts other people, *and* you could achieve that same outcome in a way that wouldn't hurt them. You know anyone who likes to always say, "I just tell it like it is," after they've said something tactlessly that could've been said differently and achieved the same effect? Well, no, sweetie, you're a fucking *asshole.* You just say whatever the fuck comes out of your mouth, and you react however the fuck you want each and every time. You are like a two-year-old who can't control themself. You could state your truth in a way that is considerate of other people's feelings with some *tact,* but you either don't have the emotional intelligence to do so, or you cannot *utilize* your emotional intelligence to hold yourself accountable and see how you come across to others. *That* makes you an asshole. Your feelings do not make you an asshole, but the *way* in which you choose to *express* them can.

Let's be clear about this: The difference between being authentically you but *not* being an asshole to others versus actually *being* an asshole is that an asshole will intentionally say things that they *know* will hurt another person. Someone who's simply living in their own authenticity without trying to be an asshole will say what they mean, drawing healthy boundaries for themselves and showing others how to do the same. They will consider whether or not what they are saying and how they are saying it will hurt someone else.

Now we understand that when we're acting as our full selves, someone *else* may call you an asshole for deciding to do something that don't make no sense to them. Being *called* one—even when you *know* you ain't hurting nobody—can really mess with our minds. It can make us backtrack. It can make us second-guess ourselves. But here's what you gotta remember, and I will say it loud and clear:

Sometimes being an asshole to people is nothing more than setting healthy boundaries.

Having boundaries is *not* the same as being an asshole. The people who might call you an asshole for putting your foot down and drawing a line will say something like "Ooh, he's not nice. Oh, she's not *nice* to me because she didn't do what I thought she should have done." Maybe I *ain't* being nice, and I don't *want* to be nice, either! Being *nice* is not a trait that I always *espouse.* I would rather you say I'm *fair.* I'm *reasonable.* I am *loving*—I get *way* more out of being those qualities than just being nice. *Nice* will set you up for being taken *advantage* of in some spaces. Having boundaries, choosing yourself over pleasing others, is a *good* thing. It is a *healthy* thing to do, and yes, it means you will disappoint people, and that's *okay.* Don't let nobody tell you different!

When people say you're being an asshole after you set boundaries, it just shows y'all that they don't know what being an asshole really *means.* They are conflating those ideas, and here's how to separate them. Being an asshole has a very *specific* connotation of being *careless* with other people's feelings. Assholes lack empathy toward other people in terms of how their ways of expressing themselves impact others. Setting healthy boundaries and dealing with the fact that some people just may not *like* your boundaries, that's not being an asshole. And if someone tries to *tell* you you're an asshole for having boundaries, that just bounces right back to them—*they're* the asshole for trying to get something out of you that will hurt *you*, that isn't beneficial to *you*.

It's one thing to have healthy boundaries, and it's *another* to think about how you communicate them. Oftentimes where we go wrong and end up in moments where we can *look* like an asshole is because we have a problem with communication, not with boundaries. It's in how we communicate and *enforce* our boundaries. Let's say your boundary is whenever a relative starts to bring the drama to family get-togethers. We all got one or more family members like that. Maybe it's your mother, your father, your kids, or your spouse, and they start to behave a little too dramatically. How you gonna react? You can react like an asshole or a non-asshole, and here's the difference.

The asshole way *rips* into whoever this particular family member is, *degrades* them, and makes them feel *less* than. It *hurts* them when you make other people feel insufficient or like less as you're communicating your boundaries. You don't *have* to communicate your boundaries in a spiteful way, but you're *choosing* to.

The non-asshole way to communicate your boundary in this scenario is by being able to step back and reevaluate. "I'm not gonna participate in this. I'm not comfortable with how you're behaving, so I'm gonna take a step back. If you'd like to come back to me later when you're a little calmer, I'm more than happy to talk then." You are communicating your boundary in a respectful way. You have not degraded anyone. You have not, in any way, made them feel less than. You have simply communicated a boundary—that you're not gonna participate in whatever drama they've cooked up—and you walked away. That is healthy and honors *your* needs without degrading the other person. It is *not* being an asshole.

When you give others your guidebook and begin to act in the way you authentically are, don't be surprised when people give you pushback, because they *will*. But remember the keys: *How* are you expressing yourself? Are your actions *disregarding* people's feelings? Or are other people simply hurt because they don't like your boundary? Stick with these questions, baby, and you'll never have to question whether you're an asshole or not again.

Take Action to Get the F*ck Out Your Own Way

If you want the quickest way to identify whether or not you're an asshole, ask yourself (or others) if you have a history of people being negatively impacted by how you express yourself. It doesn't have to be one way. You can be an asshole in almost any way.

Maybe you stonewall folks—I'm not gonna say nothing to you, not until you do this and that. Do you have a history of that? Then, yes, you're an asshole. Think about how you have talked about your past relationships with others. This is key because I have found that assholes generally have lower emotional intelligence, and you don't want to be that person! They'll say, "It was everybody else. I was the victim. My ex was just crazy. I told them the truth and people can't never handle that I'm real with them." If it's always someone else's fault, then you're the asshole. You're the problem.

Realize that the history is important because assholes are not made overnight. Nobody just wakes up an asshole. They usually have a trail behind them of broken, damaged relationships. And in the context of relationships, think about what your exes have told you about yourself.

Ask yourself if you have a pattern of victimizing yourself, blaming others, and hurting others. Be honest and be real because knowing who you really are is the only way you can get better.

18

It's Okay to Protect Yourself

We've had the conversation about self-worth, how to display ourselves to the world, and how to get over people pleasing. But for our last pep talk of this book, it's time to take that a step further: Not only is it okay to *stop* people pleasing, but it's *also* okay to protect yourself, even if it means *displeasing* other folks. We started touching on this in the last chapter, but we're about to dive in *deep* here, honey!

Assholes say to always look out for number one. People pleasers say to take care of everyone but yourself. I ain't saying either one, but here is what I *do* say: Protect yourself. That ain't the same as looking out for number one, because that includes the subtext of it being *okay* to step on others. But it's also *not* okay to let everyone walk all over *you*, so we're gonna find that fine line and learn how to walk it.

Get in here, get in here, get in *here*. We've *talked* a lot about knowing your self-worth and the steps to *achieve* better self-worth throughout this book. But let me reiterate this here: There is *nothing wrong* with protecting yourself. In fact, you *have* to protect yourself. And the way we do that is by starting with y'all's *boundaries*. We've talked about boundaries, and maybe you're sick and tired of hearing about them, but they are *that* important. Yes, you *need* them. And if y'all take only one lesson away from this book, I *pray* it will be all about boundaries, what they are, why you need them, and what the tools are to manage them effectively and appropriately. But with that said, it is my God-given *hope* that y'all take away more than one lesson.

The first step to protecting yourself is knowing that it is okay *to* do it. But the second step is to look at *how* you do it. There's a balance between the two. This means *recognizing* that you are not trying to hurt nobody; you are just taking steps to *protect* yourself. How do we think about that in terms of our boundaries?

We think about our boundaries as guardrails.

The key to good boundaries—boundaries we are *proud* of and *want* to stick to instead of ones that collapse under the pressure of caring for others—is to think of them as the guardrails in your bowling lane of life. They protect us from ending up with gutter balls, baby, which cost us time, energy, happiness, and self-worth! So think of them this way:

My boundaries are not a way to *keep* everybody out.

My boundaries are not a way to *penalize* other people for not meeting my standards.

My boundaries protect *me* from going off track and protect things from getting *onto* my track that can interfere with my path.

My boundaries are not here to hurt anybody. They are here to protect my path and your path so we can *get* to our destinations. Doesn't matter what your destination is—if it's emotional health, if it's having a great relationship with other people—your boundaries are in place to get you there, and that's it. So *stop* thinking of them as walls. They are solid, they are strong, but they are *not* just to keep others out. They are as much for *you*, to keep *you* in check, as they are for others.

Now, we're gonna talk about protecting yourself in relationships, but let me make something clear *first.* We ain't *just* talking about romantic relationships, we're talking *all* relationships. When you're trying to be selfish for good reasons by putting up healthy boundaries, that involves making some hard choices, and it applies to *every* relationship. And here's something y'all might never have realized: People can love you, and there can *still* be parts of them that are unhealthy for you to have exposure to *consistently*. Doesn't mean you don't love them. It just means that there are *limitations* on what you're willing to experience about them, and that you are *drawing* such limitations so you can avoid any awkwardness or nastiness in the future. It means that "*I* set some boundaries around what parts of you I *ain't* about, what parts of you I'm gonna say, *I'm good on that.*"

For example, a lot of parents struggle with feeling *guilty* over that fact that they have to draw boundaries with their children. And as someone raising two young adults, lemme just say that when kids become teenagers and young adults, there is a very *real* possibility that you may not always *like* these people who are in your life. Whether they're your kids or the kids of someone else close to you, you just may not always be about them, and it's *okay* for you to feel that.

Remember that you *have* to protect yourself. You do that by identifying what doesn't work for you, and *then* putting up those boundaries so that you don't have to *deal* with what doesn't work for you. You *have* to do this, or *else* you will destroy yourself.

Let me say that again: You *will* destroy yourself if you don't set healthy boundaries. Not everybody was raised knowing when to shut the door when someone else opens it for them. There are people everywhere that if they *see* an open door, they will walk through it and take *everything* out. If you give them an open door emotionally, they will come in and clear your energy out. There are people who are just draining as *fuck*. We are *literally* giving them access to us, and that means that we are gonna walk away feeling depleted and hurt. There's no such thing as *I'm just trying to be a good man. I'm trying to be a good wife. I'm trying to be a good daughter. I'm trying to be a good son.* You can't be a good *nothing* if you're not being good to yourself first.

Drawing on our newfound understanding of what it means to be needy and adding it to our newfound understanding of boundaries, let me give you *this* example of how the two go together. I have a very dear friend that fits this bill. They are *literally* the neediest person on earth. Needy to the point where if I didn't give them all of my time, they'd guilt-trip me. They were *exhausting* me. You have to understand that it doesn't *matter* how much you love someone or how much they love you, but there can be parts of people that are *unhealthy* for you to be exposed to. For this friend, it was their neediness. I could *not* deal with it anymore. I had to *protect* myself, and I had to put up boundaries after I identified their neediness as the issue. I had to make a very conscious choice about *limiting* or *eliminating* my exposure to their neediness.

In these cases, those are your two choices: limit or eliminate. I went with the first step. I was like, "I love you, but the *only* way that I can be in a healthy relationship with you is to *significantly* limit how much time I give you, so that you don't build an expectation that you should get *more* of it." They didn't like hearing that, but I *wasn't* being an asshole about it. I was simply laying down my own boundaries in a way that was not *meant* to hurt them. It was hard in the beginning. But now it has created *room* in my friend's life to have other people who are *willing* to deal with them in that particular way. I haven't *left* their life. I just limited how much of myself they get access to and stay true to *my* boundaries and what's good for me.

Protecting yourself is all about identifying what parts of that person *don't make you feel good*, and then making very conscious choices around how you can either limit or eliminate exposure to those parts of that person. If you *can't* do either, then it sometimes means figuring out how you then *end* that relationship.

No one likes the thought of ending a relationship with a longtime friend or family member. It is one of the toughest things emotionally to do. And hopefully most of the time it won't come to that. But you *need* healthy boundaries because whatever your relationship with *them* is, it is going to *heavily* impact how you interact and deal with people both *inside and outside* of your family. If you often let family off easy—*oh, that's just family, that's just how they are*—if you *continually* give family excuses to just be how they are, how you think that's gonna play out in your friendships or in your *romantic* relationships?

Not well, honey.

You'll either get in the habit of letting *other* people act the same way, too—*or* that behavior from your family members will put pressure on your *other* relationships as your friends and significant others start moving away from you because they don't want to deal with that family member's behavior that you continue to allow into your life. *That's* why you need healthy boundaries with family. It will otherwise *tarnish* how you deal with other people, and oftentimes our *biggest* emotional issues in romantic relationships *come* from the boundaries that we *fail* to set up with the people closest to us. We think we just gotta accept Mama the way she is. We just gotta *deal* with it, and like we've talked about throughout this book, that's how we learn *habits* of how to deal with those toxic behaviors. That's how we generate coping mechanisms, defensive mechanisms—that's how we learn to be emotionally unavailable, and all that other shit that have their own chapters in this book. So, *never, ever* feel guilty about putting up boundaries with family. Your family is your family because the universal God saw fit for you to be born into that bloodline. But that doesn't stop the *fact* that there may be some people in your family who, if they were *not* your family by blood, you wouldn't fuck with. They wouldn't be your friend, your colleague, your *nothing*. Realize that about your family, that just because they family don't mean you have *shit* in common.

Just because they're family don't mean you need to like them, baby. I love you, but I don't *like* you. There's more truth than we'd like to admit. It's possible that some people in your family you *don't* even love. That's a very startling thing for people to hear, I know, but it can be true. That there are people in your family that you don't even love.

Once you start thinking of it that way, then think about the reverse. That there might be people in your family who don't truly love *you*. They don't truly love you because the way they *treat* you is not reflective of love. They don't respect you. They look *down* on you, they *harm* you, they *abuse* you. They do things that are *harmful* to your well-being. Those behaviors are not indicative of someone who loves you. That person is *not* your family. Your family is anyone with whom you have both *mutually* chosen to show up for one another in a *healthy* way. *That's* family.

People say, "Blood is thicker than water." But it doesn't mean you gotta put up with abuse, neglect, or stonewalling because y'all share the same blood. Family is not something so cut-and-dried. If you're *fortunate* enough to have people that you were born into that bond with, *great.* But not everyone is that lucky. Sometimes family isn't so much who shares your blood as it is the people that we connect with through our communities, through friends—our *chosen* family rather than our blood family. If you've got friends who treat you better than your relatives treat you, *they* are your family, and ain't no one gonna tell me different. Family is not constrained by blood. Y'all remember how we said life ain't fair, it is what you make of it? Well, family is the same way. Family is whoever you *want* it to be—and it can include all of your blood relatives, or none of them. It is entirely up to you and where you draw your boundaries.

The next time you get into a situation where a family member or whoever is questioning your healthy boundary, instead of feeling guilty, do this instead:

Be real with yourself, honey! That means realizing and *naming* the people in your life that you wouldn't dare *fuck* with if they weren't part of your family. If you don't feel ready to cut them off, because that can feel and be very traumatic and isn't necessarily the best course of action in *all* circumstances, give yourself a thirty-day break.

Give yourself thirty days of *I'm not dealing with that person,* or, *I'm only dealing with them when it's 100 percent necessary.* Sometimes with family you *gotta* deal with them. An example of this would be maybe you are a single parent with kids, and you gotta see your child's parent when you drop the kids off. But *that's* where you cut it off. You ain't seeing him, her, or them other than the times you absolutely have to.

Then, at the end of the thirty days, ask yourself this: *How did it feel to* not *deal with them?*

If your answer is that it felt *better* not to deal with them, then you gotta ask yourself a follow-up: Why would you go *back* to dealing with them, then?

I know the counterargument y'all gonna have, and I'm gonna nip it right in the bud right now. You gonna open your mouth, and you gonna say, *I miss them. That must mean I want them in my life.* Even if I felt *good* not interacting with them for thirty days, I missed them too much to *not* have them in my life, or to limit my time with them significantly. Ain't that what you thinking?

Well, baby, I have news for you. That *ain't* how it works. If I *feel* more at peace, and I *feel* better when I'm *not* fucking with you, that don't mean I don't miss you. And what have I been saying throughout this book? *Don't* ignore your feelings. They are our compasses. They are the backbone to understanding our trauma, our self-worth, *everything.* I'm not saying you *don't* miss them. But if you felt *peace* during those thirty days without them, *that's* something to take a good look at.

We can miss anything that was *habitually* or *consistently* a part of our lives. There are people who miss their abusers. There are people who miss being in jail. Missing something does not mean that it was good for you or that you made the wrong decision by leaving. The only thing that matters is if your peace, your happiness, your self-worth, and your internal sense of balance during those thirty days were *greater* than they were *before* you took a step back from them. If so, then you've improved your life by not *having* that person in your life.

Let's talk about this abuser and manipulator part real quick. Y'all been waiting to talk about protecting yourself in the context of romantic relationships, so let's do it. I was sitting at dinner with my nephew-son Marco, and I came across this post to *end* all posts. This woman was writing her grievance that her *husband* was grieving his *dead mistress*. Read it again, and let it just sink in. The mistress died in an accident. But this woman only found out about the affair two days *after* the mistress's funeral—so she didn't even *know* about it before the matter!—and was all disturbed and confused about why her husband was taking it so hard. Listen, he *quit* his job, saying it was too traumatic to work. And that's not even the biggest part! The mistress was in the early weeks of pregnancy, and the husband didn't know if *he* or the mistress's *husband* was the father! I'd never heard *nothing* like this before—but let me tell you how it relates to learning to draw your own healthy boundaries of protection and letting people go even if you *miss* them.

So, this woman's husband is out of work, he's waking up during the night *crying*, and he's *also* grieving for a baby which may or may *not* have been his. She went on to say *he* told her there's no reason to be jealous or threatened *now* because his mistress is dead. He's *manipulative*. And he asked for *her* understanding *as* he grieves. As *he* takes money *out* of the household by quitting his job! Strike two—he's a *narcissist*.

Last, she asked him to visit a marriage therapist together, and you know what he said? He said he's not *ready to work on their marriage*, that he still loves the wife and never intended to leave but that he needs to see a *grief* therapist instead. A grief therapist *over* a marriage therapist? He wants to work through his grief, *not* his marriage, which means he really didn't even want to be in this marriage at all! That's why he was shacking up with somebody else and *clearly* in love with her.

This poor woman, she don't know *what* the fuck to do! She wants to be mad at him, but she's conflicted because he's in such an awful place. He's telling you out loud that he wishes she was still here, yet in the *same* breath is saying how much he loves you and never intended to leave. Well, if that woman was still alive, I'd bet anything he was gonna leave. At the end of her post, she wrote, *Do I need to give him time to mourn his loss of his mistress, or should I demand he focus on our marriage?*

This is what I said to *her* about that—then we can talk about how this relates to *you*.

I said, first of all, what the *fuck*, sis? What we need to work on is your self-esteem, right here, right *now*. It *eludes* me why you ain't taking care of yourself, why you're letting him still dominate what you do and who you care about. This is a *codependent* relationship if I've ever seen one. You're going through the shock of discovering not just an affair but that there may have been a *baby* involved. But rather than focusing on the pain that *you're* going through, you're focused on *him*. You're focused on trying not to hurt *him*. You're focused on trying not to ruffle *his* feathers. And I've got only one question: Who is there for *you*? Because it ain't him, and it sure as shit ain't you, either.

And for y'all reading this, I want you to think about this for yourself. I know we're talking about this sister's *extreme* situation, but hit pause real quick. How many situations have *you* been in where somebody has clearly hurt you, and *you're* worried about *their* feelings?

You were worried about preserving their peace. You were worried about not hurting *them*. That's *codependency*, when you're putting someone *else's* needs ahead of your own.

That's what the husband in this post was doing. When people *know* that you will put them ahead of yourself, they will *manipulate* you based on that. They will say, *I don't want to talk about this right now*, or, *I'm hurting. You have nothing to worry about*. He's doing that (a) to continue to manipulate her, and (b) so that she cannot blame him because she is literally *allowing* it.

This woman's story is just a catalyst to talk about what so

many of us have done. It is not just about her, it's about *all* of us who have put our pain in the back seat in order to be there for people who are not being there for us, family included. We will give people the sun, the moon, and the stars, and they will not give us a grain of sand when we emotionally need it.

When someone hurts you, you have a *right* to focus on you. They are no longer the priority. I don't care who they are. You have a *right* to put you first. In many cases, and in this woman's case especially, you might need some therapy. And on top of that, you might need a thirty-day hiatus, just like we talked about earlier. Sometimes you got to take a step back. You need to stay somewhere else so that you can get a clearer perspective.

In this woman's case, the husband was outright in *love* with this other woman. You sitting here worried about his feelings rather than worrying about the fact that he *betrayed* you and *lied* to you. You *found out* only after he started grieving and it *had* to come out. He was never planning to be honest with you. He was *never* caring about your feelings. We have to *stop* putting other people's feelings on a higher pedestal than we put our own feelings. I'm not trying to be cold or harsh. But I will *never* put your feelings above mine. You *don't* have a right to hurt me and then *expect* me to somehow now care about how I make you feel once I set a boundary and say *enough* is enough.

Put yourself first. If setting your proper boundaries means you gotta hurt somebody else, then, baby, do what you got to do. If standing up for you and saying *I don't want to be in this anymore, I got to take a step back* means that the other person's going to be grieving—in her case, he going to be grieving a dead mistress *and* an estranged wife—then *let them grieve.* Let these people grieve the pain that they caused in your life when you walk away and *give* yourself permission to *always* put yourself first. Forget *their* pain, put *your* feelings first.

Now, I ain't sure if part of this woman's worry was her *fear* of losing her husband, but I *assume* that was part of it. Her self-esteem was so low, she was literally caring for him *after* he betrayed her; she obviously didn't want to lose him or leave him. And here's what I say: Don't allow your fear of not *having* that person around, or your fear of missing that person, stop you from doing what you gotta do. Remember that your life was able to function *before* that person was there, and therefore it will be able to function even when they're *not* there anymore. What would happen to you if that person were to drop off the face of the earth tomorrow? How would you function after that? Thinking that you *have* to be in their life for them to be able to function is one of the greatest things that allows abusers and toxic people to *keep* space in our lives. They *know* we're more concerned about them than ourselves, and they will exploit that.

They will be just fine without you. And you will be just fine, probably *better*, without them. So let them go and focus on yourself. Change always creates pain, but you know what? It also creates *power.* And if you're not willing to go through the *pain* of letting someone go, if you're not willing to go through the *pain* that comes with setting boundaries, then you're not gonna experience the *power* on the other side of that choice. You're just gonna stay in the same cycle of toxicity, abuse, negative feelings, hurt, and pain forever. You're gonna stay there, which is also painful. That pain is *more* painful because at least the pain of changing is temporary. That pain comes from doing something different and adjusting to it. But it will eventually transform into power, and you will never know the greatness of *that power* if you don't protect yourself and learn to put yourself first.

Take Action to Get the F*ck Out Your Own Way

Let's get real with ourselves. Name the people in your life that you wouldn't even fuck with AT ALL if they weren't part of your family or in your immediate circle–if you didn't feel FORCED to deal with them.

Name them and write them down.

Then take a thirty-day break from those people, or only deal with those people when ABSOLUTELY necessary. Keep track of how you feel throughout the hiatus, and at the end, ask yourself, *How did it feel to not deal with them?*

If you felt BETTER, more at PEACE, it's time to re-evaluate your boundaries with these people. First, why would you go BACK if you're so much happier with the limited involvement? Second, how can you put up your boundaries to protect yourself? Do you just want to LIMIT your time with them, ELIMINATE it, or end the relationship?

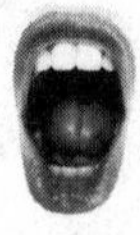

Conclusion

You Are Enough

Bring it in, get in here for the last time, everyone. The reason y'all picked up this book is because you wanted *help* in some aspect of your life. The reality is that there is too much shit everywhere that just drags us down and *perpetuates* our bitter cycles of abuse and toxicity.

But if this book has taught you anything, it's *fuck* that!

Fuck that, baby girl, and send it packing. You've already taken the first step to get better, so don't back away now. *You*, and only you, have the power to change your life and get your shit together. You, and only you, have the power to get the fuck out your own way. You already *know* you ain't living your best life, you already *know* you ain't as happy, as successful, as wealthy, as you want to be, so take what this book has been saying and *run* with it. Realize your worth and make choices to be authentic because who you are is enough.

The world puts pressure on us every day to conform, to shape-shift, and it doesn't just come from outside society—people who love us, our family, our friends, they all put pressure on us, too. And if you find success *without* being true to yourself, then it ain't your success! It's you working toward something that you're gonna be afraid of losing if people knew who you really were.

There's people out there who want you to be you but *only* in the dimensions that work for them, and that's bullshit! It'll be hard when you step out as your full self. There are gonna be people who question you, who ask you what's wrong, what's *different*. Some people might even leave your life—and you should bid them adieu, but don't lose sleep over it, because they ain't the ones who are gonna make you happy anyway. They were the ones who only liked you when you were down or weak or easy to manipulate.

You are responsible for *your* happiness. Whatever happens in your tomorrow will be based on the decisions that you make *today*, so do not underestimate the power of making good choices for your life right now. Because if you make the same choices you made yesterday, then you will experience the same kind of life you're experiencing today. And if you're trying to get your shit together and get the fuck out your own way, that ain't gonna cut it. To truly get your self-worth, happiness, inner peace, and time right, you gotta realize that nobody is going to do this shit *for* you. The person who hurts you is not going to change so that *you* can feel better; *you're* going to have to change. And then maybe they will change in order to follow suit. But they sure as hell won't take that first step unless they see *you* taking the initiative. Nothing gonna change unless you get the ball rolling. The habits and mindsets that have yet to produce a positive life for you are not gonna dramatically change what they're producing for you all of a sudden. *You* have to change the habits and mindset in order to change your own life. You are 110 percent responsible for what happens in your life, good *and* bad.

You are not a victim of life. Were you victimized at times by situations? Absolutely. But you are the direct *reflection* of the choices and mindsets that you choose to carry around *independent* of what has happened to you. There are people who've been through the same things that you've been through—*or* have been through *worse*—and are still thriving. So what's your excuse?

This may sound harsh, but I bet you will remember it, and that's what I want. Coddling each other and making each other feel as though somehow God is our personal cosmic sugar daddy who is gonna come down and make it all better for us is complete *nonsense.* At the end of the day, I believe in free will. The life that you live, and even the level of God's power that you will attract into your life, is a direct *reflection* of the conscious thoughts and the conscious behaviors that you *choose* to take on in your life. So if you wanna attract God's best, then you need to be willing to *make* the best decisions for yourself, which means taking *responsibility* for your life.

And in every choice, at *every* crossroads, at *every* point of decision, ask yourself which decision will make your life better, so you can *choose that.*

ACKNOWLEDGMENTS

Picture it: sitting in a beautiful, rustic Balinese cottage listening to the rain hit the palm trees' leaves outside the large picture window. No kids. No drama. No worries.

That's what I am doing right now as I write these acknowledgments. My life isn't perfect, but it sure is good! I finally got the fuck out my own way.

My relationship with myself is healthy; I truly love myself (flaws and all). My phone barely rings with the bullshit anymore. Why? Because I have set clear boundaries with (or blocked) the people who fuck with my peace. My health is amazing because I am now more intentional than ever about treating my body the way it deserves. Financially, well, I sure as hell ain't Oprah, but I live comfortably without the financial anxiety that once kept me up every night.

Again, my life isn't perfect, but getting the fuck out your own way isn't about having a perfect life. Perfect is boring as fuck.

It's about making the best choices that you can within your circumstances so that you can live your version of your best life. And that's what this book is here to help you do: get the fuck out your own way so that you can start making the changes that will create your best life NOW.

I want to dedicate this book to my mother, Carolyn, and grandmother Glory—the two biggest voices in my life, who constantly push me to get the fuck out my own way so that I can live my best life. They hold me accountable and love me to my core. They are my guardian angels on this earth.

I also want to thank my brothers, Charles Neal and Darren, and my sister, Nia—you've always given me the gift of reminding me that I am enough. You make me feel so safe.

I want to thank you, Dad, Charles. Your baby boy made it! Thank you for pushing me to see my "light" and share it with the world. You did good, Dad. Never forget that. And to my second mom, Dianne, thank you for always encouraging me to shine.

To my editorial team: Thank you! Full disclosure, I didn't want to do a book. I was tired and overworked, but these publishing powerhouses came together to make this possible:

Krishan Trotman, my publisher, thank you for being a visionary and exceptional leader. Thank you for motivating me.

Latoya Smith, my agent, thank you for being in my corner to make this process so seamless.

Felice Laverne, my book doula and writing collaborator, thank you for bringing out my voice. This project took us across three continents and many time zones, but we made it happen, writing this first book with laughs and positivity!

Amina Iro, Legacy Lit's assistant editor, thank you for helping to bring this work to life in such a beautiful way!

Above all, I dedicate this book to you, the reader—my "Best Friend." You're reading this book because you desire big changes in your life, and I don't take it lightly that you have placed your confidence in me to help you achieve that.

You can do it and I've got your back.

Love you,

MJ